Joint Libraries

Joint Libraries

MODELS THAT WORK

CLAIRE B. GUNNELS, SUSAN E. GREEN,
AND PATRICIA M. BUTLER

AMERICAN LIBRARY ASSOCIATION | CHICAGO 2012

Printed in the United States of America

16 15 14 13 12   5 4 3 2 1

Extensive effort has gone into ensuring the reliability of the information in this book; however, the publisher makes no warranty, express or implied, with respect to the material contained herein.

ISBNs: 978-0-8389-1138-9 (paper); 978-0-8389-9218-0 (PDF); 978-0-8389-9238-8 (ePub); 978-8389-9244-9 (Kindle). For more information on digital formats, visit the ALA Store at alastore.ala.org and select eEditions.

Library of Congress Cataloging-in-Publication Data

Gunnels, Claire B.
      Joint libraries : models that work / Claire B. Gunnels, Susan E. Green, and Patricia M. Butler.
      pages   cm
      Includes bibliographical references and index.
      ISBN 978-0-8389-1138-9
      1. Joint-use libraries—United States. I. Green, Susan E. II. Butler, Patricia M. III. Title.
      Z675.J64G86 2012
      027.473—dc23   2011044057

Cover design by Casey Bayer.
Text design in Liberation Serif and DIN typefaces.

♾This paper meets the requirements of ANSI/NISO Z39.48–1992 (Permanence of Paper).

*We dedicate this book to all the Don Quixotes
in the library world who have a vision
and the will to make it a reality.*

CONTENTS

Appendixes available for download as editable Word documents at
alaeditions.org/webextras/.

ACKNOWLEDGMENTS

Writing this book has opened our eyes to all the possibilities of partnerships, not only in libraries, but also in any endeavor. The book is the result of a partnership of sorts with the authors and our publisher, Christopher Rhodes of ALA Editions. Thank you, Chris, for the opportunity and inspiration to delve into what makes a good joint library. Many thanks to our amazing copy editor, Paul Mendelson, whose mind is like a steel trap. And thank you, Jenni Fry, our managing editor, for keeping us on track.

To those who took the time to fill out our questionnaire and e-mail us, to those who spoke to us by telephone, and to those who met us face to face, thank you for your candor, thoughts, and advice. Your generosity has helped us present a clear and up-to-date picture of today's joint library.

Thank you Pamela Anderson-Brulé, Cope Bailey, Mark Boone, Doug Caesar, Earl Campa, Patty Landers Caperton, Laura Gervais Carrion, Ryan Carstens, Enrique Chamberlain, Brad Cox, Joe Dahlstrom, Gene Damon, Ken Doherty, Ken Draves, Rhoda Goldberg, Jeff Harris, Ken Haycock, Beverly D. Hills, James Horton, Kwei-Feng Hsu, James Karney, Ruth Kifer, Jamie Knight, Audre Levy, Harriett MacDougall, Lauren Marcus, John Massey, Mary Mayer-Hennelly, Ruth McDonald, Monica Norem, James Patterson, Elaine Plotkin,

Dana Rooks, Luke Rosenberger, Clara Russell, Wendy Schneider, Dorrie Scott, Elise Sheppard, Nancy Smith, Charlie Soliz, Mick Stafford, Rachel Steiner, Julie Todaro, Diane Troyer, Darla Wegener, Bob Williams, Lyle Vance, Dawn Vogler, and a special thanks to Lamar Veatch who was willing to talk about a "glorious failure."

Last but not least, thanks to our lifelong partners, Tom Butler, Mark Green, and Stephen Gunnels.

PREFACE

This book grew out of the challenges we experienced as participants in the creation of two joint libraries. We all were founding faculty at Lone Star College. One of us, Pat Butler, was acting codirector of the Tomball Library and two of us, Susan Green and Claire Gunnels, were librarians at CyFair. Susan and Claire actually published an article about their experiences in *Community & Junior College Libraries* called "Voices from the Trenches: Librarians Reflect on the Joint-Use Library." Susan and Claire hailed from two other Lone Star colleges, North Harris and Kingwood respectively. Pat Butler previously worked in the Annandale and Manassas campus libraries at Northern Virginia Community College.

About eight years after our libraries were founded, we thought that exploring what made them work, what made some projects not work, and some interesting stories would be useful to others who are contemplating partnerships. With all the budgetary woes in the world today, saving money by reducing duplication of efforts makes partnerships not just a luxury, but sometimes a necessity for survival. Our research led us to reflect on where libraries are going and what roles librarians will have in that future. Read on to discover what we found out about joint libraries and the leaders who forged ahead.

ONE

INTRODUCTION

Access to knowledge is the superb, the supreme act
of truly great civilizations. Of all the institutions
that purport to do this, free libraries stand
virtually alone in accomplishing this mission.

—Toni Morrison

Throughout history, libraries and librarians have specialized. We have university librarians, archivists, business librarians, college librarians, collection development librarians, technology librarians, and public librarians, to name a few. While these specialties continue to exist, there is a subtle but profound shift in how libraries operate and how librarians perceive themselves. Technological changes, demographics, and economic necessity have set the stage for educational partnerships never before imagined.

One common denominator in all libraries is a mission to educate, to provide access to knowledge, and to create a place for community whether physical or virtual. Constituencies are becoming more blurred. Public libraries have classes, college libraries provide leisure reading, business libraries open doors to their community, law libraries help the researching public. Many libraries have a social presence on the Internet, in essence inviting even more constituencies to their doors. Blogs, wikis, shared catalogs, downloadable audiobooks, and e-books are examples of how libraries are growing outside their defined borders. As technology continues to evolve, nineteenth- and twentieth-century limitations on libraries have naturally begun to disappear.

This book explores the concept of interlibrary partnerships in which two or more categories of libraries join forces and create a different library with emphasis on the public/academic connection. These libraries are sometimes called joint-use libraries, dual-use libraries, blended libraries, multi-jurisdictional libraries, or joint libraries. We will agree to call them joint libraries for the purpose of this book. Joint libraries are collaborations between different types of libraries: public libraries and schools; universities and public libraries; community college and public; city and county, and more. We will paint a balanced picture of the joint library with the evidence we have accumulated. We will present examples of projects that went terribly wrong as well as examples of successful collaborations. We will spin many tales of culture shock, miscommunication, prejudices, and failed technology. Likewise, we will tell stories of success and validation. While all three of us have experience in successful collaborations, we also have witnessed fallibility and conflicts between partners. We are aware of the critics of this type of partnership—those that believe a library must specialize to promote quality control and traditional services. There are university librarians who are loath to open up doors and borrowing privileges freely to the public. There are company librarians who insist on internal-use only facilities in order to protect their corporate proprietary information from the public. There are medical and law librarians who cannot commit the resources necessary to help the public to do research. Indeed, these librarians raise legitimate obstacles and problems with the joint concept.

This book should be read by anyone contemplating collaboration: administrators, architects, lawmakers, librarians, faculty, and staff. It covers not only success and failures, but also history, technical services, collection management, library design, legal issues, staffing hurdles, operating issues, training, and quality control. See figure 1.1 for a sample of various types of joint models and figure 1.2 for a list of the main libraries in this book.

ARE PUBLIC LIBRARIES SO DIFFERENT FROM ACADEMIC LIBRARIES?

What will a library look like in ten years? How do you go about predicting the future? You can look into the past and extrapolate how things will change in the future. When philanthropist and steel magnate Andrew Carnegie gave

FIGURE 1.1
Various Organizational Models for Joint Libraries

Two-Way Partnerships

Dual employers; two directors, with one reporting to the college and one reporting to the public library

- College Hill Library, Westminster, Colorado
- Dr. Martin Luther King, Jr. Library, San Jose, California
- Lone Star College-Tomball Community Library, Tomball, Texas

Dual employers; one director hired reporting to the college

- Tidewater Community College Virginia Beach Campus Joint-Use Library, Virginia Beach, Virginia (slated to open in the first half of 2013)

Dual employers; one director hired, operated by the public library

- North Lake Community Library, Irving, Texas (This library ended up canceling the joint contract after just two years of operation.)

Dual employers, one director; position funded 50/50 and reports to both institutions

- Victoria College/University of Houston-Victoria, Victoria, Texas

Single employer; operated by the college or university

- Alvin Sherman Library, Fort Lauderdale-Davie, Florida
- Lone Star College-CyFair Harris County Branch Library, Cypress, Texas
- Seminole Library, West St. Petersburg, Florida

Single employer; operated by the public library

- Sienna Branch Library, Fort Bend County, Cinco Ranch, Texas
- Broward County North Regional Library
- Broward County South Regional Library
- Broward County Weston
- Broward County Pembroke Pines

Three or More Partners

Single employer; operated by the public library

- Broward County, Miramar Town Educational Center Library, Miramar, Florida
- Broward County Main Library, Fort Lauderdale, Florida
- Twelve Bridges Library, Lincoln, California
- University Branch, Fort Bend County Library, Sugar Land, Texas

FIGURE 1.2
Joint Libraries Highlighted in This Book

Alvin Sherman Library, Research, and Information Technology Center
Broward County and Nova Southeastern University, FL
3100 Ray Ferrero Jr. Blvd. Fort Lauderdale, Florida 33314
http://www.nova.edu/library/main/

Harmony Library at Larimer Campus
Poudre River Public Library District and the Front Range Community College, CO
4616 South Shields. Fort Collins, Colorado 80526
http://frontrange.edu/Academics/Libraries/Larimer/

LSC-CyFair Library
Lone Star College-CyFair Library, Harris County Public Library, TX
9191 Barker Cypress Road. Cypress, Texas 77433
http://www.lonestar.edu/library/

LSC-Tomball Community Library
Lone Star College-Tomball Community Library, Harris County Public Library, TX
30555 Tomball Pkwy. Tomball, Texas 77375
http://www.lonestar.edu/library/

MLK Library
Dr. Martin Luther King, Jr. Library, city of San Jose and San Jose State University, CA
150 E. San Fernando St. San Jose, California 95112
http://www.sjlibrary.org/

North Lake Community Library
City of Irving and North Lake College, Dallas County Community College District, TX
No longer operating as a joint facility

Twelve Bridges Library
Lincoln Public Library, Sierra College, and Western Placer Unified School District, CA
485 Twelve Bridges Dr. Lincoln, California 95648
http://www.libraryatlincoln.org/

University Branch, Fort Bend County Library
Fort Bend County Library, University of Houston-Sugar Land, Wharton County
    Community College, Texas
14010 University Blvd. Sugar Land, Texas 77478
http://www.fortbend.lib.tx.us/

VC/UHV Library
Victoria College and University of Houston-Victoria, Texas
2200 E. Red River. Victoria, Texas 77901
http://library.victoriacollege.edu/

Tidewater Community College Virginia Beach Campus Joint-Use Library
City of Virginia Beach and Tidewater Community College, Virginia
1788 Michael La Bouve Drive. Virginia Beach, Virginia 23453
http://www.tcc.edu/lrc

money to set up free public libraries in the late nineteenth century, his vision was one where free public libraries would be a great leveler, where even those of little means could read and learn. "Carnegie's generosity funded the development of some 3000 libraries, an incredible gift to humanity" (McMenemy 2009, 30).

Then we had the library of the twentieth century. By the mid-century, the card catalog was being replaced by microform catalogs, easily reproducible and inexpensive to create. Word processing was allowing librarians to create research guides which could easily be updated. Library consortia such as OCLC were being formed. "CD-ROMS became important information storage and delivery tools" (McMenemy 2009, 109). These were replaced by DVDs and flash drives which had many times the storage capacity. By the end of the century, libraries had discovered the Internet and a new world of shared online catalogs, cloud computing, and instant electronic delivery of information. This phenomenon was just the tip of the iceberg. The Internet would not just be shared library catalogs; it would open up a vast new world of information outside of the library. Would the library disappear? Who would need librarians when you have instant information at your fingertips? Reports of the library's death were greatly exaggerated, however. Instead, the library served as the great technological leveler where anyone could come, access the Web, get help in using computer programs, and, yes, read books.

> While they help us get online, employed and informed, librarians don't try to sell us anything. Nor do they turn around and broadcast our problems, send us spam or keep a record of our interests and needs, because no matter how savvy this profession is at navigating the online world, it clings to the old-fashioned value, privacy. They represent the best civic value out there, an army of resourceful workers that can help us compete in the world. (Johnson 2010, B9)

Thus we have seen the library evolve from a place to read and learn to a place to read and learn using technology. "The need for high quality and accurate information sources is as stark in the digital age as it was in the analogue, and the need for public libraries to ensure the public have access to definitive and well sourced reference works is crucial" (McMenemy 2009, 199). The Internet and its vast resources created new responsibilities and roles for librarians to help their communities evaluate, sift through, and utilize new information sources and connect to a global society. Technology is constantly pushing librarians in dramatically new directions and partnerships. Even the information giant Google recognizes librarians as partners in the information world. One example of this partnership is Google Books. Google has contracted with libraries of all types to scan their collections, making vast numbers of books accessible to the world.

Libraries must deal with change at an ever-increasing pace. Look at a recent phenomenon at Amazon.

> In the latest chapter in the unfolding tale of the book evolution from ink to pixels, Amazon.com said Thursday [May 19, 2011] that its customers now buy more e-books than print books. Since April 1, Amazon sold 105 books for its Kindle e-reader for every 100 hardcover and paperback books, including books without Kindle versions and excluding free e-books.
>
> "We had high hopes that this would happen eventually, but we never imagined it would happen this quickly," said Jeff Bezos, Amazon's chief executive, in a statement. "We've been selling print books for 15 years and Kindle books for less than four years." (qtd. in C. C. Miller 2011, B2).

LIBRARY OF THE FUTURE

H. G. Wells was a science fiction writer in the 1930s who used his imagination to predict what information would be in the future. He envisioned "a collaborative, decentralized repository of knowledge that would be subject to continual revision" (Schiff 2006, 3). His imagination preceded technology by many decades. However, today this sounds like the way one librarian describes Wikipedia:

> Wikipedia is a great starting point. It's a lesson in research methodology, a fun way to share expertise, and a groundbreaking new way of working. Its consensus model represents a shift in management styles and away from hierarchical organization. You might say that Wikipedia is Zen-like. Its ever-changing nature means that when you read it, you are completely in the moment. And its collective brain is like a conscious universe in which we all are one (Berinstein 2006, 26).

TECHNOLOGICAL CHANGE

For us to predict what the library of the future will look like, let's take a look at the impact of technological change and the rate of advancement throughout history. Ever since humanity invented the wheel or learned to start a fire, it kept progressing. It developed language, electronic communication, computation, data storage, and so on. Inventor and futurist Ray Kurzweil has an interesting theory regarding technological change. He believes that technology grows exponentially, not linearly. If you graph technological change over time, it starts out slowly and seemingly linearly. However, over time the curve shoots up and technology changes so fast that predictions are at best iffy. Kurzweil believes that we are presently at the "knee of the curve which is the stage at which an exponential trend becomes noticeable (Kurzweil 2005, 10). Change will happen at such an increasingly fast rate that it will be difficult to predict what the technological landscape will look like in ten or even five years.

Advances in technology are so rapid that we admit we cannot accurately describe the library of the future, but we can agree that drastic change is inevitable. Whether we like it or not, the age when a library could be self-reliant is over. To remain competitive, libraries must be ready to adapt to change and librarians need to be flexible in their outlook. They need to respond to change with imagination, enthusiasm, and open-mindedness. The new world will not wait for those who remain wedded to the nineteenth and twentieth century's, or even the last decade's, models of libraries. As in the past, libraries will be challenged to find new solutions to meet the needs of our constituencies. For example, many communities have speakers of foreign languages and need English classes. Libraries began to provide free classes by enlisting English-speaking volunteers. This type of service was unheard of in nineteenth-century America. The library had to change because its existing environment and community had changed.

A library that ignores its community, fails to marshal available resources, and is reluctant to work well with other service providers is missing an opportunity to grow and change. Sadly, in these periods of shrinking budgetary support, the library also risks its own survival. To remain significant and responsive to their communities, libraries must continue to progress by forging new linkages, partnerships, and affiliations that could be even more outlandish, groundbreaking, and beneficial to their users than the joint libraries we discuss.

After interviewing dozens of players in this arena, we hope this book will shed light on the joint public/academic library and, in the process, redefine the idea of a library. Researching for this book was a wonderful opportunity for discovery and vision. We were surprised by some outcomes and predictions of the future. We were amazed at the creativity and imagination and fortitude of all.

TWO

HISTORY OF JOINT PUBLIC AND ACADEMIC LIBRARIES

*They are the books, the arts, the academes, That
show, contain and nourish all the world.*

—William Shakespeare, *Love's Labour's Lost*

Resource sharing has been a key tradition throughout the history of libraries in the United States. For decades, larger libraries have donated earlier editions of books to smaller ones, duplicates have been traded, and reciprocal agreements have allowed borrowers to check out materials from neighboring library systems. Libraries have willingly spread their resources beyond their local boundaries by sharing items in their collections with faraway strangers via free or low-cost interlibrary loans. Yet, until recent years, libraries have been averse to the idea of taking the next step in the evolution of resource sharing—jointly operating with a different type of library under one roof.

More than forty-five years ago, the federal government began to exert its influence on academic libraries through legislation that encouraged them to combine their physical locations as a way of "strengthening their developing institutions." The administration of President Lyndon Johnson pushed the Higher Education Act of 1965 through Congress with its provisions for federal grants for "joint use of facilities such as libraries and laboratories including necessary books materials and equipment" (P.L. 89–329, sec. 304). Despite this legislation, higher education officials were slow to investigate how and where to share libraries. During the 1960s and 1970s more attention was paid by universities on how to team up with industries to lower the cost of expensive research laboratories than on working with their academic rivals to merge libraries. State government agencies dealing with an influx of college-age baby boomers were also interested in controlling the costs of higher education. To limit duplication of services, the states put tight controls on new graduate or professional degree-granting programs so that they would not compete with existing degree programs in the same geographic areas and also designated non-overlapping service area boundaries for the fast-growing community college systems. Instead of consolidating libraries, colleges and universities, for the most part, spent the two decades following the passage of the Higher Education Act constructing larger and larger libraries—and even multiple libraries on some university campuses. In this "grow and you will be rewarded" era, academic libraries were in a competitive race with peer institutions for boasting rights on which institution could house the most volumes. There were a few exceptions, such as the joint library in Texas between Victoria College and the University of Houston-Victoria, established in 1973, and the triple-partnership Auraria Library which opened in 1977 and is shared by the Community College of Denver, the Metropolitan State College of Denver, and the University of Colorado-Denver. But for the most part, the predominant goal of academic libraries and their parent institutions was to grow independently. They were not alone. School districts and public library systems placed similar premiums on retaining their autonomy and self-sufficiency.

SHARING COSTS

Perceptions about sharing infrastructure costs started to shift in the late 1960s due to the large outlay of funds required to convert from manual to automated library management systems (Bostick 2001). Library professionals agreed that they got a better price by negotiating a single contract for new systems or by pooling their resources and piggybacking on automation systems run by larger libraries. Small library systems which could not afford to hire their own technical support personnel were thrilled when a state agency or large institution stepped in and took over the responsibilities for purchasing, installing, and hosting the system and sent them a pro-rated bill. The advantages of having shared catalogs and single hosting sites were soon apparent. They sped up the processing of new materials, brought standardization to catalog descriptions, gave users an up-to-date record of their own institution's holdings, plus let them easily peek at what was available in surrounding libraries. College, government, and library administrators realized that these joint projects favorably affected their bottom lines because they were able to significantly lower both their infrastructure expenditures and their personnel costs for the technical squads needed to run the servers, create the networks, and write the programs that allowed for customization. The interdependent automation systems also generated the formation of "user groups" which influenced attitudes about sharing and generated the open exchange of newfound solutions and the voluntary adoption of best practices among peer institutions.

SCHOOL/PUBLIC LIBRARY EXPERIENCE

Although a number of jointly funded school/public libraries were established in Minnesota, Wisconsin, Colorado, and Utah, most libraries rejected the idea of implementing a hybrid library model because of the overwhelming challenges of dealing with what they saw as their inherent differences. Library administrators generally did not think it was feasible or cost-effective to try to mesh staffs with different credentials and skill sets, revamp their systems to match another platform, inflict new operating routines and hours on their users, conform to varying fiscal regulations and calendars, deal with two governing authorities, or take on the stressful responsibilities of effectively serving additional library constituencies on a daily basis (Bundy 2003; Wisconsin 1998; State Library of Iowa 2006). In addition to emphasizing their differences, opinions on joint libraries leaned toward the worst-case scenarios: no one would feel welcomed, the materials would be hoarded by the other partner's users, the facilities would be inadequately staffed and overcrowded, and the peace and tranquility so many sought in a library would be invaded (McNicol 2006). A few expressed their deepest personal fear—they would no longer have complete control over their library. While libraries applauded the advantages of interdependence and multiple levels of resource sharing of materials and technology, they moved quickly to try and block any recommendations for combining their physical facilities. Numerous guidelines for joint school/ public libraries were published by central library agencies. The guidelines from the Queensland, Australia Department of Education (1996) and the State of Wisconsin (1998) forewarned those contemplating a joint library to only move forward after reconsidering all of the obstacles, and offered very few positive outcomes for what was described as a risky endeavor. A united front in opposition to the idea of joint school/public libraries was evident. The New

Jersey Association of School Librarians and the New Jersey Library Association, along with the New Jersey State Library (2003), developed standards for joint school/public libraries, but the document actually presented their strongly held feelings of why such facilities would not work in their highly populated state. The two associations instead proposed that it was a better use of taxpayer funds for libraries to plan "joint projects—not joint facilities" (New Jersey Library Association 2002, sec. Public Libraries and School Libraries). The State Library of Iowa updated its guidelines on joint use libraries in 2006 and again provided detailed checklists of the "obstacles" involved and prominently shaded text boxes with statements that clearly discouraged the pursuit of a joint library option (State Library of Iowa 2006, 3).

Except in California, support for joint school/public libraries continued to shrink across the country. In Wisconsin's 1998 report, only six shared libraries were listed. In the 2002 draft of the revised guidelines for Wisconsin (Hennen 2002, 2, 13), a shift toward the successful combination of municipal libraries with twenty-three such facilities was evident, but there were still only six combined school/public libraries. In Iowa's revised publication in 2006, only twelve school/public libraries, one community college/public library, and one private college/public library were listed (State Library of Iowa 2006, appendix B, 23). The Institute of Museum and Library Services' statistics for public libraries in 2008 indicated that 1.5 percent of the 9,221 public libraries in the United States were in the category "Other," which included combined school/public libraries (Henderson et al. 2011, 43, table V). The most dramatic reversal of support for combined libraries can be seen in Minnesota's Library Development and Services Report in 2000, which listed over 100 previously combined libraries, but showed that only two joint school/public libraries remained in existence (appendix B1). Numerous state school media library associations and public library associations continued to declare the concept of shared library facilities as unrealistic due to their distinct differences in missions. The findings that the Canadian experience with joint libraries was equally disappointing strengthened their opposition. According to Alan Bundy (2003), it was widely believed and repeated that joint libraries could only work in a rural area that serviced a small population. Some combined libraries were presented as a temporary solution until the area became more populated and the public library or school system could afford its own facility. Both Bundy and Sarah McNicol (2006) found that there were often feelings that outsiders were not welcomed in the combined facilities located on school grounds or that it was inconvenient for the community users to wait until the school day was over to use the library. There were also frequent complaints that in school/public libraries the materials were mainly for children and did not have sufficient materials for the full range of adult reading. The low usage rates by community members and the higher-than-expected operating costs persuaded the public library systems and the school systems to quietly discontinue their jointly operated experiments and return to the traditional independent library models.

CONSORTIA INTERDEPENDENCE

By the 1980s new consortia and regional library groups evolved as more libraries investigated ways to make cutting-edge technology feasible and affordable in their institutions. Collaboration among college and university libraries in the United States expanded, but the efforts were limited, by and large, to technical services or back office activities such as automated systems, cataloging, group purchases, and licensing of online databases. As the technology continued to rapidly change, collective purchases multiplied for such things as optic cabling, modems, personal computers, CD-ROM servers, microfiche duplicators, and more robust integrated library management systems. There was an upward trend of different types and sizes of libraries clamoring to join the "members-only" buying clubs so they too could stretch their limited funds by taking advantage of group discounts when purchasing big-ticket items. For the most part, the new purchasing relationships retained the traditional segregation of the different library peer groups. The top-tier research institutions stuck together, and the community colleges and private universities formed their own consortia, as did the school and public libraries. However, as Sharon Bostick noted, once their technological needs were satisfied, the academic research library consortia moved into a new direction toward shared collection development responsibilities in subject areas where materials were difficult or extraordinarily expensive to acquire (Bostick 2001). Since expansion space for libraries on university campuses was more and more limited and increasingly expensive, the research libraries were cajoled into identifying infrequently used materials that could be stored in jointly funded off-site facilities. Despite initial misgivings, sending materials to low-cost off-site storage facilities became an accepted practice and gave research libraries the breathing space they needed to enlarge their collections while balancing the expectations of faculty to have the research materials readily available. The success of off-site storage gradually triggered new ideas about the sharing of preservation responsibilities among nearby libraries. Librarians willingly collaborated to develop equitable remedies for reducing the number of duplicate titles as they became keenly aware of the considerable overlap in their holdings. These new collection development and preservation partnerships were seen as risky by some, and even radical by faculty who wanted everything at their fingertips, but, in hindsight, they seemed rather conventional in comparison to the daring construction of combined public/academic libraries that began in Florida in the 1980s.

FLORIDA'S PIONEERING JOINT LIBRARIES

Despite the negative results for school/public library partnerships, the idea of combining libraries continued to intrigue both political leaders who continuously juggled more requests for funds than they could fulfill and taxpayers who wanted their property tax dollars stretched as far as possible (Florida Postsecondary Education Planning Commission 1999). The huge population boom that occurred in Florida, after the opening of Disney World in 1971, challenged the state and local governments to quickly provide an array of new educational and civic facilities and services. Government officials began to investigate ways to reduce capital, operating, and technology costs by building shared facilities and multi–institutional-type centers for higher education. In 1983 the Broward County Public Library and what was then known as Broward Community College (now Broward College) broke with the tradition of building stand-alone libraries by combining an academic and public library on the south campus of the community college. This highly publicized library challenged the accepted norm of who should have the responsibility for operating libraries. The library was situated on the college campus, but it was the Broward County Public Library System that ran the facility and employed the staff. Just four years later, the academic library management paradigm was nudged again when the main library branch of the Broward County Library, built as part of the revitalization plan for the downtown Fort Lauderdale area, entered into a three-way agreement with Florida International University and Florida Atlantic University. In this location, the public library would not only provide reference and research services to community users but also to the faculty and students who attended classes at the nearby University Tower. Buoyed by the success of its first joint partnership on the south campus, the Broward County Public Library and the Broward Community College opened a second joint library on the college's new north campus in 1994 (Broward County Library System 2010). Again, it was the Broward County Library that operated and staffed the facility.

Broward Community College continued to see the benefits associated with shared facilities and joined forces with Florida Atlantic University and Florida International University (which later moved its classes to another site) to begin planning a new library on its central campus, known as the Davie Campus. Anthony Trezza was hired as a consultant to help develop recommendations for an integrated library, staff, and services in this new $14 million facility. Trezza's recommendations led to the formation of a governing policy/advisory committee with representatives of each institution, a determination that the best operating structure would be for all of the library staff to be college employees, and an initial funding formula with the community college providing 60 percent and Florida Atlantic University 40 percent (J. Woods 2001).

Broward College was not the only college experimenting with joint libraries with university and public partners. Brevard College began sharing a library, known as the Clark Maxwell Lifelong Learning Center, with the University of Central Florida on its Cocoa Campus in 1984. These two academic institutions had the advantage of a long history of partnerships dating back to 1968 when the university and the college (then respectively named Florida Technological University and Brevard Community College) established a Center for Continuing Education on the college's campus. The college and university also had worked closely together to establish an articulation agreement that was later replicated at community colleges and universities throughout the state so that students could complete an associate's degree program at the community colleges and easily transfer to a bachelor's degree program at the nearby facilities of the state universities. Instead of one entity being the primary partner at the Clark Maxwell Center, a joint policy board determined how the library was to operate and a "common library card was issued to borrowers of both institutions" (Florida Postsecondary Education Commission 1999, 19).

In December 1999 Nova Southeastern University (NSU), the largest private university in the southeastern United States and long recognized as a pioneering leader in providing innovative graduate and distance education programs, boldly challenged conventional library roles by entering into a forty-year formal agreement with the Broward County Public Library System to build the state-of-the-art Research and Information Technology Center. The library, which is now known as the Alvin Sherman Library, cost $43 million and opened in 2001. It is the largest library in the state of Florida with 325,000 square feet, as well as the largest public/private library in the United States. According to the profile submitted by NSU for the *Chronicle of Higher Education*'s Campus Viewpoints (Nova Southeastern University 2011), the five-story library was intentionally designed to break new territory:

> The idea was to build a facility large enough, diverse enough, and technologically advanced enough to provide the right information for the right person at the right time. Library supporters planned for a hub where

residents, business people, students, and scholars of all ages and interests would have access to information in the library or from their home computers.

A year after opening, John Lubans (2002) interviewed Don Riggs, the NSU vice president of information services and university librarian, to get an insider's view of the "extraordinary benefits" for each of the partners. Riggs felt that the county library system benefited by having a technologically advanced library with hundreds of computers and wireless connectivity, a convenient location that offered county residents access to both research and public library collections, and longer operating hours. The benefits that the joint library brought to the university were the fulfillments of the university's mission to serve the community, a new academic library enhanced by the addition of the public library collection, and additional operating funds for the building and the collections. Lubans reported that "county funding support will range from 40–50% of operating expenses each year. And the Broward County Board of County Commissioners has committed $5 million for new books" (Lubans, 2002, 176–78).

Although the Alvin Sherman Library could claim to be the first public/private academic library partnership in Florida, the first such facility in the United States was the Cole Library on the Cornell College campus in Mount Vernon, Iowa. This small private college offered the community of Mount Vernon joint use of its library through a "gentleman's agreement" dating back to 1905 (Cole Library 2011). This joint venture, which has lasted for more than four generations, eventually had to be formalized (according to Cornell College's website in 2001) because the Cole Library needed to be officially designated as a public library to take advantage of additional state and county funding.

SPREADING MOVEMENT

Although Florida was getting most of the press coverage for opening joint academic/public libraries, by the mid-1990s other states were also getting on the bandwagon. The idea of having one facility that served both the college and the community was no longer viewed as a sea change—but more as an evolutionary change. Rappahannock Community College's Warsaw Campus agreed in 1993 to provide library services for the rural community of Richmond County, Virginia. The informal agreement between the college and the county was formalized five years later in a written contract in order to designate the college librarian as the certified public librarian. This action enabled the county to remain eligible for funding from the State Library of Virginia (Richmond County Public Library 1998).

Colorado had proven since 1977, with the earlier mentioned Auraria Library, that higher education projects could be built faster and at a lower cost by combining college and university programs in a single location. In the early 1990s the City of Westminster and the Front Range Community College were both developing their own plans to build new libraries within miles of each other. At the urging of their top administrators, representatives of both libraries visited the two joint libraries on Broward County College's campuses and investigated several other models, to determine if a joint public/academic library option was viable for their institutions. Rather than duplicating the examples they had seen in Broward County with a single entity running the joint library, a dual management system was selected for the College Hill Library. Aware that this decision added layers of complexity, the two staffs began to closely communicate even before the 76,000-square-foot College Hill Library opened in 1998 on the Westminster Campus. In order to make the new library accessible to all the people it intended to serve, the teams concentrated on eliminating any unnecessary competition and duplication and closely aligning their internal systems (Sullivan et al. 2006, 569–70). Front Range College also partnered with the City of Fort Collins and opened a second joint 30,000-square-foot library in 1998, aptly named the Harmony Library, on its Larimer Campus. As with the College Hill Library, the land and building are owned by the state of Colorado. The fiscal responsibilities outlined in the Colorado Commission on Higher Education's Master Plan (Stubbs and Carlson 2007, 4) indicate that in this partnership agreement, the "college is responsible for the facilities costs while the city is responsible for the daily operational costs, including the librarians." The harmonious library relationship continued even after the City of Fort Collins transferred all of its responsibilities for the library to the newly formed Fort Collins Regional Library District (2007), now known as the Poudre River Public Library District.

Besides the historic joint library partnership at the Cole Library between Cornell College and the community of Mount Vernon, there is a second and much different academic/public library in Iowa. The Iowa Lakes Community College's Emmetsburg Campus Library and the Emmetsburg Public Library are located in a building on the college's campus that also houses a shared wellness center for the city, county, and college. Since 1997 the two library systems have shared the building and an online catalog, but each library operates on different floors and explicitly retains its own identity and governing boards. Although the two Emmetsburg libraries have been established as colocated libraries, the achievements listed on the Emmetsburg, Iowa, website are similar to the goals of an integrated joint library:

> It provided more spaces, handicap accessibility, expanded services, study and leisure reading space, work space for staff, and more programming opportunities. It also provided access to materials for both students and the public and eliminated a lot of duplication. (Matthews 2009, para.2).

The first academic/public library in Indiana opened in 2002. The 35,000-square-foot library on Ivy Tech Community College's main campus in Lafayette was constructed and furnished by the Tippecanoe County Public Library. The final paragraph in the joint use proposal for the Tippecanoe County/Ivy Tech Library (2002) indicates the following positive outcomes for each of the partners:

> For the public library, the cost of building and operating additional space would be higher without the financial contribution possible through the proposed partnership. For the college, capital funds are difficult to obtain. The provision of capital funding by the library will allow the college to stretch its scarce capital resources in exchange for ongoing operating support. For both institutions, enhanced services, longer service hours, an augmented collection, materials, and electronic resources will be possible through the combining of the resources of the two institutions.

In the joint Tippecanoe library, the college contracts with the public library for an initial period of twenty years to operate the library and provide technical services while the college covers the building and maintenance. The staff is shared, except the public library is responsible for staffing the children's services and the college provides the staff needed to support the college's curriculum.

Back in Florida, joint libraries continued to emerge. Soon after the opening of the Seminole Campus of St. Petersburg College, the City of Seminole and the college began thinking about cooperatively working together to build a community library. Although it took years of public debate, the City of Seminole and St. Petersburg College entered into a formal agreement in October 2000 for the design, construction, and operation of a $6.8 million, 52,000-square-foot joint library. The anticipated benefits of this joint project were increased access to advanced technology for both the college and the community and the maximum use of tax dollars. The joint project, located on the St. Petersburg College's Seminole Campus, opened in August 2003, just across the street from the existing city library location. Following the organizational model of the first two Broward College/Broward County library partnerships, St. Petersburg College is responsible for maintenance, security, utilities fees, and the technology while the city is in charge of the library's daily operations and personnel (Olliver and Anderson 2001).

St. Petersburg College continued to ride the joint library wave. A new 50,000-square-foot library was opened in 2005 in Pinellas County on the college's Gibbs Campus after more than three years of collaboration and planning between the city of St. Petersburg and the college. This partnership involved unusually complicated personnel issues because it replaced the Azalea Library, which had for years been a combined public/school library. All of the Azalea Library's school employees, with the exception of one who retired, decided to move over to the new library and become college employees instead of being transferred to other school facilities. Patricia Bauer's (2006) study found that many of the school employees made their choice to move to the new college-run library because they wanted to stay together as a team. Although they had experience working in a combined library and were familiar with many of their colleagues, many found the transition unsettling in the new West St. Petersburg Community Library. The former school district employees faced a very different reporting structure, varied work schedules, and additional requirements for cross-training to learn both the college's and the public library's systems. As Bauer pointed out, avoiding tensions and conflicts among the staff and creating a new standard for customer service required significant communication and attention during the opening year.

Despite economic downturns that led to extensive budget cuts for the Broward County Library Division and strained the county's relationship with Nova Southeastern University over contractual obligations for the Alvin Sherman Library, the county library, Broward College, and NSU developed a new three-way partnership that culminated in the 2008 opening of the Miramar Education Center. In this new three-story Miramar Town Center facility, the county library operates the library, which serves the constituencies of all three entities on the first floor, and the college and the university utilize the upper two floors for their academic course offerings.

Since the last decade of the twentieth century, Florida has continued to embrace joint library projects as a natural part of its centralized planning for higher education and frequent practice of building collocated colleges and universities. Seminole State College and the University of Central Florida (UCF) dedicated a joint use library in March 2010 in the new Partnership Center complex. UCF is currently planning another joint use facility with Valencia College which would bring its number of shared university/ community college library facilities to five. UCF's other three partnerships are with Daytona Beach Community College at the Daytona Beach Campus, Brevard Community College at Palm Bay, and Cooper Memorial Library, a joint library with Lake County and Lake Sumter Community College at South Lake. In addition to the UCF facilities, other joint college/university libraries in Florida include Lakeland Campus Library (a partnership with Polk Community College and the University of South Florida) and Fort Walton Beach Campus Library (a joint venture of Okaloosa Walton Community College and the University of West Florida). There are also several other public/college/ university joint libraries in Florida: the Jane Bancroft Cook Library (a joint use facility for the New College of Florida, the University of South Florida– Sarasota/Manatee campus, and residents of the counties of Manatee and Sarasota), and Indian River St. Lucie West/Florida Atlantic University Treasure Coast Campus Library (a combined library for Florida Atlantic University, Indian River Community College, and the St. Lucie County Library System).

Following Florida's lead, libraries in Texas started to experiment with joint libraries—not in rural areas but in the largest metropolitan areas in the state—Dallas and Houston. Both of these cities and their surrounding counties saw exploding populations, rapid residential developments, and soaring property and sales tax revenues in the late 1990s and early 2000s. In a move that was aimed at meeting both the college's enrollment projects and the heavy demands on the public library system, North Lake College, one of the seven colleges that make up the Dallas Community College District, and the City of Irving agreed to build a new joint 55,000-square-foot library on the college's main campus. As discussed in the case studies in this book, the North Lake Community Library venture was not long lasting due to a mismatch in expectations and lack of internal support to continue the shaky relationship. The decision to reestablish separate libraries took time, enormous public relations efforts, and additional expenditures to divide up the materials, such as the costs associated with "reprocessing over 60,000 items" by the City of Irving Public Library's technical services staff (City of Irving 2005, 18). The library director, Lyle Vance, commented, "When we decided to call it quits, I had to learn to deconstruct a library. I didn't learn that in library school" (Lyle Vance, pers. comm.).

In 2000 the North Harris Montgomery Community College District (now known as Lone Star College) began planning a comprehensive campus in the far northwest portion of Harris County (which surrounds the City of Houston). The campus was being designed by the newly appointed college president, Diane Troyer, and a small staff using a "process that pulled input from various sectors of the Cy-Fair community to determine what educational, technological, cultural and social classes, programs and facilities the college should offer to meet the needs of the community" (Cy-Fair Houston Chamber of Commerce 2008, para. 9). The college's strong commitment to community collaboration made this the perfect place and time for Harris County's Precinct Three commissioner, Steve Radack, to spearhead an agreement between the college district and the county library system to build a joint 78,500-square-foot library that would serve the college and learners of all ages. The CyFair joint library created what Radack felt was "the opportunity to offer everyone a library with more amenities, more features and more services" (Canyon Gate Communities 2004, para. 7). The new comprehensive Cy-Fair College Campus and the joint library opened with great fanfare in the fall of 2003. Despite its immediate acceptance locally, it was still unknown how the college's accrediting agencies would view the public/academic library facility. The college administrators were relieved when they received the following feedback from the review committee for the Southern Association of Colleges and Schools:

> Cy-Fair College is commended for the collaboration and integrated model it has designed and successfully implemented for its library, and more exclusively, its Learning Commons. Planned jointly with the Harris County Public Library system and Cy-Fair College, the Learning Commons is already a model of integrated learning that expands the concept of community and makes seamless, indeed interchangeable, the roles of the teacher and learner.
>
> The learning space brings together a wide array of student support services, knowledgeable staff, state-of-the-art technology and collaborative stewardship of state, local and federal funds to redefine for all of us the true meaning of "community" in community colleges. (qtd. in Park, Murray and Campa 2007, slide 19)

Less than fifteen miles away from the Cy-Fair Campus, the North Harris Montgomery Community College District had another campus, Tomball College, which was getting ready to expand its library in 2002, along with several other campus facilities. These internal plans were put on hold when it was learned that the Harris County Public Library System was going to have to abandon its proposed replacement library in the City of Tomball due to drainage problems on the site. Due to this turn of events, instead of building two new libraries just a few miles apart, the decision was made by the college president and county commissioner to build a joint library on the Tomball College Campus. As reported in newspaper articles (Downing 2002), the decision was highly unpopular with area senior citizens and members of the Friends of the Library, as well as some faculty, but the resistance faded when the architecturally stunning 72,000-square-foot building opened in January 2005. It was surprising to some that the organizational and management structure for the Tomball joint library was different than the one that had been adopted at the college district and county's first joint library in CyFair. Because the CyFair Library had only been open a very short time and because two existing libraries were being brought together in Tomball, the decision was made to adopt a dual management system like the one Tomball's planning committee had seen at the College Hill Library in Westminster, Colorado. (See the Tomball case study for more details.) Although the Harris County Public Library and Lone Star College are convinced that joint libraries are tremendously beneficial to both organizations, financial difficulties due to reductions in property tax revenues have put a third joint library facility planned by these two partners for the North Harris Campus on hold until the economic situation improves.

Just a few years after the Lone Star College joint libraries opened, nearby Fort Bend County Library opened the Sienna Branch Library in April 2010, in Missouri City, Texas, as its first joint public/college library. The library is a two-story, 45,000-square-foot building on a 4.5-acre site next to Houston Community College's Southwest-Missouri City Campus. The building is operated and staffed by the public library, but approximately 10,000 square feet of the library is designated for the college's use, plus a college librarian is employed to specifically meet the needs of the community college's students. The Fort Bend County Public Library System operates a second shared library facility, the University Branch, which opened in November 2011 in Sugar Land, Texas. This new library is situated on the shared satellite campus for the University of Houston System and Wharton County Junior College. At this location, the Fort Bend County Public Library System will again hire the staff and operate the University Branch Library that will serve the community, the university's faculty and students, as well as the students and faculty of the junior college. (More information on the University Branch is in the case studies.)

CALIFORNIA RESHAPES THE JOINT LIBRARY CONCEPT

Of all the joint academic/public libraries in the country, the one that received the most notice and faced the greatest skepticism about its future success was the Dr. Martin Luther King, Jr. (MLK) Library in San Jose, California. The joint library project for the San Jose Public Library and the San Jose State University was first proposed in 1997 and took six years and over $177 million to complete. When the possibility of a joint library was first announced there were organized rallies to try and save San Jose State University from what many saw as a forced marriage with the public library. On the other side, the public library system was heavily criticized for committing too much money to an extravagant downtown location at the expense of its heavily used suburban branches (Eanes 2010). The joint library, however, had a unique third partner, the San Jose Redevelopment Agency, a powerful agency that was blessed with deep pockets filled with tax revenues from the technology boom and which coveted the existing public library site for an expansion of the convention center as part of its plan for the revitalization of the downtown area (Berry 2004). A deal was struck with the two libraries because the redevelopment agency had a convenient site available that was adjacent to the university and, even more important, it could issue capital bonds for the new library because the site was in the revitalization zone. An additional factor in moving the project forward was that the redevelopment agency could be designated as a financial partner, which would make the university's request for additional capital funds from the state system a higher priority. Both the university and the public library endured the internal and external criticism and several near derailments because each had a need for a larger library and both were facing critically unmet technology needs in their current facilities. As the university president Robert Caret expressed in his announcement, both the university and the city came to realize that together "we can achieve what neither institution could accomplish by itself" (qtd. in Eanes 2010, 47).

The synergistic relationship in San Jose did not come easily. In the detailed planning process of building the new library and developing the "prenuptial" agreement that would govern the new facilities, the two libraries had to closely reexamine their own operating systems and become creative in developing a new interdependent framework. According to the San Jose city librarian, Jane Light, they did not want a duplex library with only the "sharing of a wall and no sharing of services"; instead they used multidisciplinary teams to find new and innovative solutions that would sustain the partnership (Light 2008, video).

While the San Jose joint library was capturing attention around the country and internationally because of the size and price of the project, California's public libraries, school districts, and community colleges were also developing an array of new and innovative joint library operating models. The incentive behind these new partnerships was the passage of Proposition 14, the California Reading and Literacy Improvement and Public Library Construction and Renovation Bond Act of 2000, which gave first priority for funding to public library construction requests that had cooperative agreements in place with one or more schools. As an example, the 2000 North Natomas Library cooperative agreement between the City of Sacramento, the Sacramento Public Library Authority, the Natomas Unified School District, and the Los Rios Community College District came about because the school district and the college district built a new high school and community college facilities on land adjacent to the public library site in the Town Center Educational Complex. Instead of each educational unit constructing and maintaining its own library, both chose instead to partner with the public library. The additional funding allowed the public library to nearly double the square footage of the original proposed facility from 12,000 square feet to 23,000 square feet and to be open 15–20 more hours per week than other branches in the public library system. The added space gave the library enough room to add a computer center, adult literacy program, a career center, a distance learning center, gallery space, and community service opportunities for high school students (City of Sacramento et al. 2000). Anne Marie Gold, the director of the Sacramento Public Library Authority, credited the success of this joint library on the fact that it was part of a new planned community and "because the library director, the high school principal, and the college president get together for coffee every Monday morning" (Martin and Kenney 2004, sec. Learning Library).

The new focus on reduction of taxpayer costs and economic efficiency in government in the state of California clearly changed perceptions and made joint use projects an acceptable community practice:

> Priority shall be given to proposals for new joint-use centers institutions where the State of California is relieved of all or part of the financial burden. When such proposals include gifts of land, construction costs, or equipment, a higher priority shall be granted to such projects than to projects where all costs are borne by the State, assuming all other criteria listed above are satisfied. (California Postsecondary Education Commission 2011, sec. on economic efficiency)

Another joint library that emerged after the passage of Proposition 14 and that was also part of a master planned community is the 39,100-square-foot Lincoln Public Library at Twelve Bridges, a cooperative effort of the City of Lincoln (2003), Sierra College, and Western Placer Unified School District that opened in late

2007. The new emphasis on cost savings is highlighted in the Twelve Bridges Library case study by Francesca Wright, who reported that the partnership "will result in a 67% reduction in administrative overhead for the City, a 30% reduction in over-head costs, and a 50% increase in library hours of operation" (Wright 2005, 2).

The Lafayette Library and Learning Center in California propelled the idea of a joint library into a new universe when it opened in 2009 as a new and larger library for the Lafayette community, but also as the home for the Glenn Seaborg Learning Consortium. Instead of sharing library collections, this 30,000-square-foot library and learning center notes on its foundation's web page (Lafayette Library 2011) that it shares its venue with the twelve educa-tion, science, and art partners in the consortium: the California Shakespeare Theater, the Chabot Space and Science Center, the Commonwealth Club of California, the Greenbelt Alliance, John F. Kennedy University, the John Muir Health System, the Lindsay Wildlife Museum, the Oakland Museum, the Oakland Zoo, Saint Mary's College, the University of California's Institute of Governmental Studies, and the Lawrence Hall of Science. Each partner commits to providing at least four programs, exhibits, children's activities, workshops, films, lectures, and so on per year. They are also obligated to pro-mote the programs of the other consortium members and the library on their own websites. Besides providing the facility, the library foundation furthers the collaboration by providing volunteers, a consortium calendar, links on its website, and a newsletter to attract audiences of all ages to the wealth of enrichment offerings (Urban Libraries Council 2010).

TROUBLING TIMES

The University of Washington-Bothell (UWB) and Cascadia Community College (CCC) in Washington State have shared a campus as well as a library since 2000. The conflicts between the two institutions on how the campus should operate and be funded have been manageable, but nevertheless have led to strained relations over the years. As one official described the nego-tiations between the top administrators over who should pay for what, "For awhile there, it was like watching two porcupines making love" (Trombley and Irving 2001, 10). In 2009 the future of the joint library and the joint campus in Bothell was uncertain. The university pushed for legislation that would have resulted in a merger between Cascadia Community College and Lake Wash-ington Technical College which basically would have evicted the community college from the campus, thus allowing the university the use of the entire campus for its own enrollment (Shupe 2009). By the spring of 2010, talk of relocating Cascadia Community College faded after the legislative request calling for a study of the possible merger of the community college and the technical college was withdrawn from the budget. Despite the squabbling in the upper echelons, the single library, referred to as the Campus Library, has from its beginning days gone out of its way to break down institutional barriers. Before the campus opened, the decision was made that the library would be run by the university because it had ten years' experience operating the library in another temporary location. Although the community college members have the benefit of accessing a much larger collection than a typical community college library, the privileges at the Campus Library are strikingly different for UWB and CCC faculty and students. A major reason for the differences is that early in the negotiations both parties agreed that one institution would not subsidize services for the other (Fugate 2001). Cascadia has paid twice as much as other community colleges for library services at Bothell, but that is still not a large enough contribution for equal service levels with university users. UWB students can place holds on materials at other locations via the online catalog, while CCC students cannot. Interlibrary loan is free for UWB, but CCC users pay a fee. Courier delivery from other University of Washington campuses is available for UWB borrowers, but CCC users have to visit those libraries in person if they want to borrow an item (University of Washington Bothell 2011).

The situation in Bothell contrasts sharply with the recent agreement between Coconino Community College and Northern Arizona University. The small community college was forced to close its library in the summer of 2010 in order to deal with dramatic budget cuts. The college's president and the nearby Northern Arizona University president reached an agreement that would allow the community college's students and faculty to use the university's Cline Library. Not only did the community college users get access to a library with more materials, longer hours, and reference assistance, but the agreement also included remote access to databases and interlibrary loan and document delivery services. The plan is for the community college to compensate the university based on tracked college usage. Instead of marking territorial boundaries, already the two institutions have started more in-depth discussions on other ways to join forces and leverage their purchasing power, such as the licensing of online databases. The news announcement on the college's website (Coconino Community College 2010, para. 6) quoted the university president, John Haeger: "With higher education budgets continuing to be squeezed, this has the potential to serve as a model for other institutions seeking creative solutions to shrinking budgets."

The downturn in the economy is creating an impetus across the country for new multi-type libraries or entirely new library models that have broader missions and serve new constituencies. Scott Walter studied the motivation behind emerging multi-type libraries in his discussion of what was then a proposal for Wayne State University to take over the financially troubled Macomb County Library. Walter describes Wayne State University as wanting to more actively fulfill its mission of civic engagement by sharing its library school expertise with the financially strapped public library system and, secondarily, achieving its strategic objectives to attract more college students from Macomb County (Walter 2010). The takeover was approved, and in 2009 Wayne State University assumed responsibility for providing library services to the citizens of Macomb County, as well as students from Macomb Community College, Wayne State University, Baker College, and area high schools. The 25-year lease with Wayne State stipulates that the university would take over the library's building and maintenance and provide essential library services. According to an April 18, 2009, article written by Maureen Feighan in the *Detroit News:* "The deal maintains the library, but not as it is now. No materials will be lent, and only a portion of it will be open to the public to use computers and reference materials." The deal did allow the public library employees to be retained in the renamed Macomb County Reference and Research Center until they quit or retired, but Wayne State University is under no obligation to fill these positions once they are vacated. To control costs the library was transformed into an electronic library and the existing book collection was donated to other area libraries. Walter predicts that this is also an opportunity for what had been a traditional library to become more actively engaged in the concerns of the community and meet the "dual imperatives of the library to advocate for its significance to the campus, and of the campus to advocate for its significance to the community" (Walter 2010, 8).

The first joint public/academic libraries came about because there were visionaries who were willing to take risks to expand services and share resources outside the traditional library lines. More recent joint libraries have emerged as a survival strategy to operate as cost-effectively as possible and withstand prolonged budget shortfalls. The shared libraries highlighted in this chapter are just a sampling of the joint public/academic libraries that have been attempted. In reviewing these libraries, it is clear that continuous flexibility and ongoing collaboration were key requirements for their longevity. It is also apparent that no single organizational model works best. Even within the same library systems, different approaches have been taken because each library, location, and partner needed to weigh its own distinct needs and available funding possibilities. One thing is certain: the novelty and naiveté surrounding joint libraries is wearing off, which makes the path to success easier for those that follow. There are still risks, and the agreements are still incredibly painful to negotiate and difficult at times to adhere to. From a historical perspective, joint library partnerships, on one hand, have been great opportunities for libraries to make their mark and draw new users. On the other hand, joint libraries are fast becoming a savvy strategy for maintaining strong public support in an era of diminishing funding and relentless changes in technology.

THREE

CULTURE CLASH BETWEEN ACADEMIC AND PUBLIC LIBRARY EMPLOYEES

*We can't solve problems using the same kind
of thinking we used when we created them.*

—Albert Einstein

Creating a joint library requires combining two or more different constituencies. It might be a university library and a
community college. It might be a community college and a
public library. It might be all three. It might be many other
combinations of societies, community centers, and schools.
In this chapter we will explore one combination: academic
and public libraries.

In the past, academic and public libraries were very different in their mission and operation. Academic libraries
were created to serve their own faculty and students and
to facilitate research. Public libraries were created to allow
educational resources to flow to a community with generous
donations and tax dollars. Compare the Harvard University
Library with the Cambridge Public Library. The hallowed
halls of Harvard seldom saw a community learner, and rarely
did a Harvard student venture outside of the quad to visit the
public library teeming with children, popular fiction, and
magazine browsers. The public library would host ethnic
festivals for the community, conduct business seminars,
and promote readers' advisory services. The public library

was noisy while the university library was staid and quiet. Public librarians answered reference questions such as "What is the population of Boston?" and academic librarians would assist faculty in doing scholarly research and teach students the elements of the research process.

These may seem to be stereotypes, but to some extent, these two cultures still exist in libraries today. In its feasibility analysis, the Tidewater Community College (TCC) speculates on whether "one facility can truly support the missions of a Community College and a Public Library. The underlying concern is that in trying to serve all, the core missions of the institutions might be diluted and no one will truly benefit" (Virginia Beach 2005, 13). It concluded that if both entities are truly collaborative and not competitive, "each user group will have access to much more than one organization could ever provide alone." The TCC president, Deborah DiCroce, said that there were challenges in merging academic culture with public library culture. "We are not looking to create yours, mine and ours" (Wagner 2009, B2).

The deputy director of the Poudre River Public Library District in Colorado, Ken Draves, writes about how public/community college collaborations are ideal:

> A public/community college joint use library is an especially good combination. The missions and the service populations are similar enough to provide significant overlap and allow for excellent services to all users. For example, community college students find that the public library's collections of materials and resources meet many of their academic needs and provide an excellent complement to the materials owned by the college. Likewise, community college students respond well to the friendly service orientation provided by a well-trained public library reference staff. I think that other combinations, such as a high school/PL or university/PL joint use library, present additional challenges to good service that we do not face. (Ken Draves, pers. comm.)

(Harmony Library at Larimer Campus is a joint operation with Front Range Community College and the Poudre River Public Library District.)

MERGING CULTURES

Once the two cultures are merged during a joint venture, there can be some radical adjustments that must be made by the librarians and staff of each type of library. What is a joint library's mission? To educate, yes. To expand horizons, yes. To help with research, yes.

There are legitimate cultural differences in these two types of libraries. It is a good manager who can harness the best of both worlds. Instead of saying, this is how the public library does this, have the librarians say, what is the best way to do it for our library? Let's explore some of the cultural differences in these types of libraries.

Facilities

Most public libraries have restrooms separate for staff. Most college libraries don't. Public libraries with open access can draw a messy and sometimes destructive clientele. There are homeless people and some troublemakers who deface restrooms with tools and effluvia of all sorts. Children will have accidents and have sticky fingers. Rarely does a college library have these kinds of problems. It may be a culture shock for academic librarians to have to clean a bathroom or children's accidents.

Treatment

Public libraries treat their librarians differently than academic librarians. Public libraries have a hierarchical structure, whereas many academic librarians are faculty and are accorded a strong say in how things are run. Public librarians are the worker bees who often have strict dress codes and rigid time constraints on their day. Academic librarians are responsible to other faculty for curricular needs, and they are encouraged to publish and innovate in their teaching. Some academic librarians can be shocked when the public library management treats them like the typing pool as opposed to a valued faculty member.

Some faculty are concerned that public librarians do not have the experience in teaching that an academic librarian has. In the past, some librarians chose public librarianship because they are not comfortable teaching a class. This is really not the case anymore since public librarians now teach computer classes and even English as a Second Language classes. In a joint library it's important to have flexible staff who can learn teaching techniques and how to conduct programs for adults, teens, and children.

Filtering

Academic librarians abhor filtering of computers. They believe this is an invasion of intellectual freedom. Public libraries routinely filter computers for pornography and even social media. A joint library will have to find a happy medium, perhaps just filter children's computers. Another option would be to offer filtering to parents who need it, but leave most computers free to access any website. At Lone Star College-Montgomery in Conroe, Texas, there was no filtering in this college library. A citizens' group caused an uproar when they accused the library of offering pornography. All libraries can be targets of interest group criticism if they do not filter.

Collection

Centralized purchasing of materials is usual for many public libraries. The administration orders all the books with minimum input from librarians. Academic librarians purchase all of their materials to support the curriculum. It can be disturbing for academic librarians to give up control of what the collection will look like.

Programs

Adult, teen, and children's programs are an important part of public library services. Public librarians have experience creating a diverse series of educational and recreational activities for all ages. Academic librarians usually limit their programs to teaching students. Librarians in joint facilities need to learn to do both. Joint libraries offer all librarians an amazing variety of activities which require imagination and creativity as well as academic credentials.

"Once a public librarian, always a public librarian" is a cliché which unfortunately can be accurate in describing professional career options. College and university librarians, as well, are hesitant to cross over or leave the academic career track for career opportunities. If an academic librarian joins a joint facility, it may be difficult to be hired in any other academic library, especially those with tenure and requirements to publish. In addition, reference assistants are commonly part of the public library landscape. These are usually college-degreed staff who perform many of the routine duties of a master's-degreed librarian. They work the reference desk, do programs, give tours, plan events, and do outreach such as retirement home book clubs, and so on. Some academic librarians might balk at nonlibrarians performing these functions.

TWO DIRECTORS, TWO PAYROLLS, TWO CULTURES—ONE HAPPY STORY

Lone Star College-Tomball Community Library is a joint library with Harris County Public Library, in Houston, Texas. With two codirectors and separate staff, this endeavor started out with two cultures not particularly cooperating nor truly partnering as a joint library should.

One of the unplanned things that changed the culture at Tomball and quickly integrated the public library employees into the college's culture and rhythm was the location of the library at the front entrance of the college. The library parking lot was the first one spotted and made the first floor of the library the gateway/unofficial information desk for first-time visitors to the campus. Committed to providing the best customer service, the public library employees embraced this new role and familiarized themselves with the layout of the campus; the location and hours for admissions, the business office, conference rooms, the testing center and the bookstore; the college's web page; the faculty phone directory; and the daily schedule of college events. Other things that made them feel a part of the campus included being invited to all the ceremonies, performances, and special events sponsored by the college and having the same perks as college employees, such as free access to the campus wellness center and discounts at the bookstore.

Rug Rats

Harmony Library of Colorado, a joint public and community college library, had a director with a shock of her own. "Inevitably the reality of a joint use library will not match the expectations partners have prior to opening, despite the best efforts to plan carefully. For instance, I know that the initial campus librarian was distressed by the sheer popularity of the library when it opened, and in particular the numbers of children. Her previous experience had been in the much smaller, quieter, and less busy college library, and she was surprised and displeased by what she considered the overwhelming use by the public and especially by children and their caregivers. Ultimately she retired, and the new campus librarian came in with much different expectations and a robust appreciation for working together for the benefit of all members of our joint-use service community" (Draves, pers. comm.). This highlights the fact that staff buy-in is important to overcome culture shock in a joint venture.

North Lake Divorce

Often decisions to create a joint library come from leaders in the community who see a need or an opportunity to improve services in an innovative way. Sometimes the leadership changes or the goals are not adequately conveyed to the worker bees (librarians). The Irving Public Library director and the president of North Lake College became acquainted with each other while serving on the library board of directors. This creative duo came up with the idea to create a joint library. As you will see in the chapter of this book on case studies, failure to integrate staff at the grass roots was one of the downfalls of this library. Additionally, when these leaders moved on to other positions, the impetus for success weakened.

Save Our University Library!

SOUL was the buzzword on the campus at the San Jose State University. Save our university library! What an uproar from faculty when the leaders of the university and of the city of San Jose proposed a joint library. Fears of faculty not having access to research materials and of students crowded out of computer labs were rampant among the college staff. Secretly, librarians wondered how this project would actually work. In the case studies chapter of this book, we discuss this famous Dr. Martin Luther King, Jr. Library and the bumpy road before the cultures were successfully merged.

What Culture Clash?

Some librarians beg to differ. A library is a library is a library. Dana Rooks, dean of libraries at the University of Houston, trusts the public library of Fort Bend County, Texas, to run a branch serving university students and Wharton County Junior College students as well as the public. In fact, Dean Rooks wanted the public library to run the facility and to that end mandated that current academic librarians working at the Sugar Land campus would not be grandfathered in but would need to reapply for a new position if they wanted to work for the new joint library. This way they could hire librarians who truly bought into the idea of a joint facility run by the public library. Their hope was that there would be no culture clash if the right mix of librarians with the right attitude was hired (Dana Rooks, pers. comm.). The university and the college also committed to paying the county library a sufficient sum of money to acquire materials to support their curricula and to hire librarians who could teach research skills to their students. In essence, this facility will be a large, beautiful public library with public librarians serving all constituencies. Whether this is a trend in joint libraries or an anomaly is discussed in the case studies chapter.

IS IT WORTH IT?

Most joint library ventures will not fire current employees and require them to reapply for a job in a new joint library. Thus, there usually is some culture adjustment required for all employees. During the planning process, managers must weigh the pros and cons to ensure that both sides will benefit equally. In the case studies chapter, we will analyze new ventures and discuss our chosen predictors of success. Some libraries, after conducting feasibility studies, decide not to proceed. The intrepid few who do proceed must face more challenges. In the next few chapters we will review management, design, legal considerations, collection development, and technical services.

FOUR

MANAGEMENT AND HUMAN RESOURCES

When you believe something can be done, really
believe, your mind will find the ways to do it.

—Dr. David Schwartz, author
of *The Magic of Thinking Big*

Nearly every library will say in some fashion or another "Our people are our most valuable resource." Certainly, staffing is one of the largest, if not the largest item, in the budget. Like every resource, it must be properly administered and developed. There are a variety of issues that make the management of a joint library different from other libraries. *Management* in this case is referring specifically to the overseeing of the library and the library staff. Additionally, there are consequences for departments that also affect the library, and these will be discussed.

If the employees are hired by two separate entities, there will be issues between the two partners, some of which were detailed in the section on culture clashes. When the library is under one management, there is still the necessity of serving the needs of different patrons which may conflict on occasion. If the joint library includes at least one existing library, there will likely be staff that was hired before the joint agreement was decided, and there are specific issues that develop with merging staff. It will be useful to draw up the two organizational charts and see where the various positions relate to each other. However, if one has the opportunity to hire staff specifically for the new entity, there are certain elements to be taken into consideration.

HIRING FOR THE JOINT LIBRARY

Each and every new hire knows in advance that he or she will be working in a joint library. It is essential that everyone be committed to the joint concept and to assisting all types of patrons. Library employees who have worked at either type of library may feel uneasy or even have negative connotations of the other type. It is important to discover how they have interacted with patrons in the regular setting of their own library. In the interview, it is best to ask them behavioral questions: What have you done?—not What would you do? Some other examples are: How do you as a public librarian ordinarily assist college students? How do you as an academic librarian interact with the public? Part of this process is for the candidates to elaborate on their experiences serving a variety of patrons (even if only occasionally) and realize that in any interaction their focus is on meeting the customer's needs. Of course, in asking such questions, one can determine if the potential employee, in fact, does not have a strong sense of customer service. Particular biases would be exposed and hopefully identified as either insurmountable (and thus not a good candidate) or workable. It may be useful to ask how the candidate has handled situations in which two sets of priorities were in conflict to see how she juggled opposing demands.

There is a tendency to look for applicants who have worked at both types of libraries, but the pool of such candidates is not large. This can be particularly difficult at the director level. The search committee for the director of the Lone Star College-CyFair Library (LSC-CyFair) reported that there was a small pool of candidates, as the public partner requested the director have public library experience. Therefore it may be more realistic to look for strong candidates who understand the goal of the library and are sincerely excited by the challenges and benefits. Harriett MacDougall, the executive director of the Alvin B. Sherman Library at Nova Southeastern University, says that "if it was not possible to find both types of library experience, the search committee looked for librarians with a desire to work with both types of user groups. Traditionally, public librarians respond to reference inquiries with an 'answer' and academic librarians teach users how to find the answer. In this new joint use library, the plan was to find a blend of the two approaches—to give the answer as needed and to encourage further learning with a high service attitude and an engaging environment in which to learn library skills" (MacDougall and Quinlan 2001, 145).

At LSC-CyFair, all the librarians hired for the adult reference desk had to be willing to teach research instruction classes to students. In the initial hiring phase, however, only the specifically designated instruction librarian (who coordinates and oversees instruction requests from faculty) had to teach a class as part of the interview process. The interview process was later changed so that all reference librarians had to demonstrate their teaching ability, since all the librarians teach classes. The concern was voiced that candidates with public library experience would be at a disadvantage because they would not have a curriculum-based example, but the decision was made that they could demonstrate a computer class or other type of presentation so that the committee would have a sense of their instructional style. At the new University Branch, the current job description for reference librarians at Fort Bend County requires that the librarians teach computer and database instruction classes. It is felt that these qualifications also cover the ability to teach basic library orientation for college classes.

Most joint libraries have expanded service hours. In the interview process, the fact that employees of the joint library will have different hours and holidays than other locations/departments of either parent organization will need to be mentioned. This disparity is a particular concern when the staff is hired by different employers, but it may also be a concern even when the entire staff in the library works for the same entity. One example is a joint library located on an academic campus that is open during Christmas break or spring break when other parts of the campus are closed. Some type of consideration will need to be given to employees working during this traditionally closed period. For example, at LSC-CyFair, during the times that the campus is closed, there is an attempt to have as many hours as possible covered by part-time employees, and full-time employees who work are given compensatory time. On the other hand, having employees from different entities may be a benefit in that staff may be able to cover the library during each other's holidays. This is the procedure at the Dr. Martin Luther King, Jr. Library in San Jose (Kauppila and Russell 2003, 263).

There are additional challenges to managing a joint library if the employees are hired by different employers and have different pay scales and evaluation criteria. These differences are more problematic and less easy to resolve. However, in some cases the reason the two libraries did not merge their staffs is that employees of each entity were entrenched in a particular retirement system and would have lost benefits in switching systems. The employees will need to bear this factor in mind. This was the case at LSC-Tomball, for example, and despite the disparity, this was not a particularly contentious point.

At LSC-Tomball there was an uncomfortable disparity between some employees being paid and some not for time when the campus was closed due to hurricane damage. This is covered in detail in the case studies chapter's section on LSC-Tomball. Such points as a uniform inclement weather policy are the sort of thing that probably did not come up during the negotiation process but did become an issue later. It is impossible to plan for everything, but the commitment by management to being fair to all staff should assist in getting through difficult patches. Other factors may be such points as paying for parking.

MERGING STAFFS

The West St. Petersburg Library switched from being a collaboration between the City of St. Petersburg and the Azalea Middle School Library to a joint library with the city and St. Petersburg College. Staff who had been employed by the school district became new college employees. As such, they were then subject to the six-month probationary period. Although potentially stressful for staff, this gave the director flexibility to ensure everyone was adapting to the new mission.

Some of the joint libraries that merged existing libraries spent a long time developing work teams that coordinated the various processes, such as inter-library loan or collection development. The development of new procedures is essential to smooth operations, but the team-building benefits are also essential because they enable the staff to see "how the other half lives" and also recognize their similarities. Employees get to know each other in a work setting and gauge work styles and processes.

The new teams may want to perform some specific team-building exercises, such as completing a "team-building diagnostic" which will give the group some ideas of how they may work together. When working together, they should designate a clear purpose, develop specific agendas, and get coaching as needed. They may also perform team-building exercises such as those in *Quick Teambuilding Activities for Busy Managers: 50 Exercises That Get Results in Just 15 Minutes* by Brian Cole Miller. Conducting a quick exercise at the beginning of some of the meetings will allow the participants to get to know each other better and develop more trust in each other. However, it is important that participants can see the value in the exercises rather than viewing them as merely a way to kill time. The goal is that these activities provide a learning experience in working together.

Formal training is vitally important. Even if there are not merged libraries, it may be beneficial for new librarians to shadow someone at each partner's existing locations. This is in addition to attending whatever training both institutions offer. At the West St. Petersburg Library, after the basic training for the circulation desk staff, "every new staff member would have an experienced college partner when they worked circulation in the first six weeks on the job" (Bauer 2006, 592). At Nova Southeastern's library, the librarians hired for the new library toured all the partners' college libraries as well as Broward County's Main Library in the downtown area of Fort Lauderdale. They attended sessions on all the databases they would now be using (MacDougall and Quinlan 2001).

Depending on the size of the library staffs, comparing organizational charts and developing a new one may be a major endeavor or not. At the MLK library, consultants met with library staff and held focus groups with both institutions to "design an organizational structure that would maximize the two institutions' strengths and create efficiencies that enabled the same number of staff to provide new and improved services in a much larger building" (Breivik, Budd, and Woods 2005, 402). However, even in a smaller setting, it is important to formally see how responsibilities and services line up. There may be redundancies or gaps. There may be services that one library has a librarian performing that may be handled by circulation staff in another. These points should be clarified before the library opens.

EVALUATIONS

If all librarians are hired by the academic partner, as is the case in the LSC-CyFair location, there are now new types of librarians—children's and teen librarians. This difference means that job descriptions and performance evaluations must be tweaked. For job descriptions, the changes were easily adapted from the public library.

Performance evaluations were a bit more problematic. College librarians, in addition to their reference, instructional, and collection development responsibilities, are expected to perform institutional service and closely interact with faculty. Although there is a temptation to see children's and teen librarians as purely serving public patrons, it is important to recognize every employee's contribution to the success of a joint library. Children's librarians serve on committees in the college as do adult services librarians. At LSC-CyFair, institutional service encompasses serving on committees in the public library system as well as on the campus. It is not stated in the evaluation description as such, but librarians are reminded of this point and encouraged to list services performed for both entities. The evaluation form for librarians at LSC-CyFair is the same one used across the college district, where the other librarians are all academic librarians. The form prompts the librarians to explain how they have met the following goal: "Demonstrates teaching effectiveness in the classroom and at the reference desk." At CyFair the evaluations take into account that learning facilitation applies to conducting children's story times and hosting teen book clubs as well as the more traditional reference desk and information literacy activities aimed at college students.

For all the positions, it is important to take into consideration that the new mission is different from either partner's original mission, and evaluations need to reflect that duality. Individual goals should reflect a commitment to improving services and assisting all types of patrons. It is important to highlight whenever possible how the academic community may be helped by public programs or services and vice versa. Particularly for employees who have only worked in one type of library previously, there may be a temptation to stay within one's usual sphere of duties. All of the employees should be judged on their performance in meeting the shared goals.

In libraries where personnel are employed by different institutions, it is important that performance evaluations get input from the other partner. At the MLK library in San Jose

> the agreed upon process calls for evaluations to be done by each employee's own institution with oral input from appropriate personnel. Once the performance evaluation is written, it becomes a confidential document and cannot be shown to a supervisor or team leader from the other institution. It is important that all employees be trained in the difference between the two processes and supervisors from the other institution have clear guidelines for how to give input to the evaluation process of the other party in accordance with union contracts and according to institutional guidelines. (Breivik, Budd, and Woods 2005, 402)

GOAL SETTING AND STAFFING

As mentioned, it is important for management to ensure everyone has a strong sense of the mission of the library. Every employee must "buy in" to the idea of the joint library. As mentioned in the chapter "Culture Clash," even one employee who is not enthusiastic about the idea can cause an array of problems to spread. It is best to promptly discuss in a nonconfrontational way the concerns of the questioning members. As with any personnel issue, if divisive issues are left unresolved they rarely go away but continue to fester. The management and the staff all need to take the attitude that problems are workable and that they will work together to solve any problems that arise.

The priorities of the library should be recognized and formalized in a way so that when scheduling conflicts arise everyone has a starting point for resolving the issues. As an example, the top priorities of the reference staff in an academic library may be listed as assisting patrons at the reference desk and teaching library instruction classes. If the priorities are clear, adequate coverage at the reference desk and the scheduled classes is verified before librarians are assigned to cover additional programs. If there is a scheduling conflict between offering additional programs and a pressing need for reference desk coverage or prior commitments for library instruction classes, the other programs will need to be sacrificed. In a joint library operated by the public library, the priorities may be different, with children's programming, for example, taking precedence over other activities. It is imperative that the top priorities reflect the dual mission. This is not to say that the top priorities will always remain the same—it is important to periodically revisit them, particularly if there have been staffing changes or changes due to external factors.

Some librarians may question why someone would want to work at such a library. Potentially there is the confusion and uncertainty of working in a new setting. The benefit for employees working in a joint library is the sense of working with something new and different. There is the mental growth of answering different types of questions, which happens continuously at a joint library. Most of the librarians report enjoying these challenges. One librarian described the process of creating the joint library as "the most exciting time in my professional career" (Ruth McDonald, pers. comm.). In staffing the library it is important to find people who are excited about the prospects and allow them to explore the new ways that a joint library can develop.

LIBRARY DIRECTORS

All good partnerships require good communication. Library directors of joint libraries are usually at the nexus: they are the key means to keep information flowing between both entities. It can be a difficult balancing act to report to two bosses and meet the expectations of both parties. The library director at Lone Star College-CyFair Branch, Mick Stafford, often has to mediate when two policies are different. "When policies don't match up, choose the one which balances the community's interest with the college's. For example, with fines, we agreed not to give staff any fines for overdue books" (Michael D. Stafford, pers. comm.).

It's important to have a director who can see both sides. At North Lake Community Library in Irving, Texas, the director was a public librarian. He instituted policies which clearly would not work in a college library. For example, the library required two weeks' notice for a bibliographic instruction session. In fact, the public library tried to introduce generic bibliographic instruction rather than teach a class with a particular assignment or discipline in mind. Both policies clearly did not meet the expectations of faculty and students. According to the former library manager, Lyle Vance, the library also restricted use of the computers to two one-hour sessions (Lyle Vance, pers. comm.). Student research often requires longer uninterrupted hours.

The joint library director must also guard against territoriality on the part of the staff. Cross-training between departments can break down any such barriers:

- Train librarians to check out books
- Have the children's staff learn the basics of the adult reference desk
- Allow reference librarians to do story times if so desired
- Encourage participation in both public library programs and college-type activities such as classroom teaching.

Joe Dahlstrom, director of the Victoria College/University of Houston-Victoria Library, says that dealing with two institutions is exciting and every day is a learning experience. Tongue in cheek, he also said he has to go to twice the meetings (Joe Dahlstrom, pers. comm.). At LSC-CyFair the director must attend the monthly Harris County Public Library (HCPL) library director meetings and the monthly college director meetings.

At LSC-CyFair all library employees report to one director who then reports directly to the vice president of student success. As part of the LSC-CyFair contract, there is a steering committee composed of the college president, the vice president of student success, the library director, and the HCPL director which is scheduled to meet quarterly and resolve library conflicts. These meetings would serve as a way for the public library to have input into library decisions. However, as time has gone by and confidence in the library and the staff has strengthened, these meetings have become less frequent. The library director contacts each side independently as concerns arise and acts as an intermediary. The director makes decisions with consideration of both points of view. Since the library is a seamless model, there is no sense of "on the academic side we will do this and on the public side we will do this." Generally, however, the director contacts his direct supervisor first, since if someone had a complaint about a decision he made the complainant's next step would be the vice president. Then the public library is informed, except in the case of circulation questions, which are sent to the public library first.

For libraries with dual administrators, complaints would be handled directly up their usual chain of supervision, with the added notification of their co-director. Obviously some complaints or issues lend themselves more easily to one administration or the other. The governing structure of the partners may dictate how and what information should be reported. Much of this reporting will be little different in a joint library than it would be in another library, just duplicated.

ISSUES FOR ADMINISTRATORS

In drafting the joint agreement, the primary focus is on the building, the collections, and the staff. However, there are secondary factors that must be discussed and planned for. These factors have costs associated with them that may affect the agreement and the budget for the library. These factors include security, building maintenance, custodial services, landscaping, and computers and computer infrastructure. Computers and computer infrastructure are covered in the technology chapter.

Security

The importance of security is related to the size and location of the library. Typically an academic location will have some type of security in the form of campus police officers or security guards. It is also customary for large public library facilities to hire security firms for the safety of their customers and employees and the security of the materials and equipment. Now that the public and academic library are sharing space, there may be different patron issues than the library or college campus is accustomed to, such as how to deal with homeless people, unattended children, or foul-mouthed students. The library staff may be unprepared for handling such complaints, vary in their tolerance levels and methods for dealing with inappropriate behaviors, and be unsure at what point higher authorities or law enforcement/security officers need to be brought into the situation. This ambiguity may also apply to other staff on campus who are not library employees but who interact regularly in the library.

In a joint library operated by an academic component, students who are behaving inappropriately in the library may be referred to campus resources such as counselors. The consequences for more serious misbehavior may be a referral to the dean of student services and handled as a discipline issue or even expulsion. Serious complaints about a public patron, however, would have to be handled in another manner. In a joint library operated by the public library entity, the branch manager would need to decide if the students or public patrons should be banned from the library as part of a criminal trespass order if they present an ongoing problem. In joint libraries with dual management systems, there should be written policies on how and who should address these types of problems so that there is consistency in responses to complaints and also in the treatment of offenders.

While complaints about noise are probably an issue in any type of library, the dynamics of the public/academic library may lead to more complaints. Many people have the perception that an academic library will be a quiet space. The library management will have to decide how much effort should go to monitoring and responding to noise levels as well as a general response to noise complaints.

The library staff might not be the only ones that need to work special schedules. Managers of joint library facilities must keep their security forces, technology staff, and custodial teams informed of special operating hours that will require their services, during winter or spring breaks for instance. Joint libraries on college campuses have the added concern of making sure the entry points to connecting buildings are securely closed off during these time periods. The library codirectors at LSC-Tomball learned the hard way that not everyone pays attention to the library's published library hours. During the first major holiday closure for the college after the joint library opened, the library staff arrived to work the regularly scheduled hours, but they could not enter the building because all of the electronic key card entrances had been programmed not to let anyone in until the whole campus was scheduled to reopen. After some delay in tracking down the lone security guard, they entered the building only to discover that the heating, ventilation, and air conditioning (HVAC) system for the entire campus was also turned off and the facilities personnel who could turn it back on were out of town. After that incident, there were multiple reminders sent before each holiday to the department heads and administrative assistants for the campus police, technology support, custodial services, and facilities maintenance to make sure all library systems were up and running whenever the library was open.

A joint library on a community college or commuter university campus may actually attract more unattended children during the summer and school holidays than usual because faculty, staff, and students who are parents may feel that the library is a safe place where they can leave their children while they work or attend class. It is useful for librarians, particularly children's librarians, to be able to communicate to parents what the legitimate options are to leave their children, such as campus or nearby day care facilities. It is helpful if the guidelines for leaving unattended children in the library are posted and communicated. It may be necessary for the library management team to talk to the campus human resources department, student services administrators, and nearby schools to enlist their help in communicating to parents why leaving their children alone in the library is not a good idea and explain other opportunities. It is important for the library staff to be vigilant toward problem patrons. If patrons feel the library does not have the proper ambience they may either not use the library or withdraw their support. All patrons need to have the perception that the library welcomes them and is responsive to their concerns if these issues should arise.

FACILITIES MANAGEMENT

Consideration must be given to the fact that joint library users are more numerous and thus create greater wear and tear. As the activity level in the library increases, so does the need for higher levels of custodial service and repairs. Responsibilities for custodial service depend on the "ownership" of the building and what arrangements were made in the legal agreement between the partners. In the case of the Lone Star joint libraries, the buildings are college facilities and custodians are college employees. In the case of the University Branch of Fort Bend County, the building itself is owned by Fort Bend County so it is serviced and maintained by the county. Managers in charge of joint library facilities may witness shorter life spans for computers, printers, chairs, and flooring due to heavier than expected use and will need to keep their funding authorities aware of furniture and equipment that need to be replaced.

The supply budget can also evaporate faster than expected. Although there were over 150 public access computers at the LSC-Tomball Community Library, they were in constant use. Large portions of the supply budget had to unexpectedly be allocated to the frequent replacement of the computer mice and mouse pads. The staff was also constantly searching for ways to secure comfortable but durable headphones that were unattractive enough not to go home with the users.

Directors of joint library facilities come to quickly realize that adequate and accessible parking can be one of the major factors in their success. They frequently hear complaints from patrons, particularly seniors or those with young children, about the long walking distances to the library or that they have to circle the lot endlessly. The demand for student parking may fluctuate. Designated spaces would be problematic. The College Hill Library in Westminster added an additional parking lot of 150 spaces after the library had been open less than a year due to the overcrowding (Sullivan et al. 2006, 576). In the plans for the University Branch of Fort Bend, additional parking has already been added.

Landscaping of the area around the library and the parking lots will also need to be negotiated in the legal agreement. In the case of a public library located on the academic campus, there will have to be consideration for the fact that families with young children will now be more active on the campus. A last-minute design feature caused the LSC-Tomball library codirectors real concerns. The architects added a second-floor outdoor balcony and the codirectors worried about toddlers and other young children being on the balcony without adult supervision or standing on the furniture and leaning over the edge. The issue was avoided for a little while because the library first opened in the winter months and the balcony door was kept locked at all times. Later in the warmer months, the facilities department added super-heavy wrought iron furniture and umbrella stands to the balcony area, which prompted lots of requests to leave the balcony open. As it turned out, the railings were high enough to avoid any mishaps, the furniture weighed too much to budge, and the glass door was too heavy for small children to open on their own. The balcony door was also in the direct line of sight for the second-floor reference desk, which made it easier for the staff to keep a watchful eye on who and how the balcony was being used.

BENEFITS FROM JOINT LIBRARIES

Administrators of joint libraries do have more than their share of complications and problems. However, it might be useful to review some of the benefits of joint libraries.

Just as there are some costs to the campus that occur from the joint library on campus, there are also benefits. Having families coming regularly to the public library should lead to increased awareness of campus activities. The Lone Star College system offers a summer program for children called Discovery College. Since the first year, the program has been wildly successful, whereas at other campuses it took a few years for the program to become completely full. It was felt that this was partially contributable to the success of the children's library programs. LSC-CyFair also has a successful seniors program titled Academy for Lifelong Learning (ALL). The library offers a daytime program called LIFE which has developed a core group of seniors who attend events at the college, many of whom became the first advisory board for the ALL group. Many of these same people volunteer for the arts department and serve on the board for the arts outreach. When the college district was conducting focus groups for the bond election, it was relatively simple to get a group of community members who were familiar with the campus in the group who attended LIFE programs.

Similarly, the wide variety of programs offered by the joint library at Nova Southeastern University has attracted large numbers of people to the campus, with over 28,000 patrons attending approximately 1,000 programs held between June 2002 and July 2003 (Marie 2007, 25). The attendance of diverse groups may also assist in getting grants for the library or other organizations on campus.

The MLK library in San Jose has provided a bridge between the university and the greater community. "Perhaps the most significant and intangible benefit of the library partnership is that it healed the sometimes stormy relationship the university had with the city for many years. Today, collaboration has replaced estrangement between the two parties and they are discussing future joint ventures" (Marie 2007, 26–27).

WORTH IT?

We asked a former vice president of LSC-CyFair, Earl Campa, whether he would do another joint project. "Definitely. In fact, if we hadn't followed through on this joint library, this would be a travesty for both students and public alike" (Earl Campa, pers. comm.). He saw that students would miss being exposed to such vast resources of the public library, and rarely would the community be so enriched by the vibrant and open campus.

FIVE

DESIGN OF
JOINT LIBRARIES

*I have always imagined that Paradise
will be a kind of library.*

—Jorge Luis Borges

The process of designing a new home for the joint library
is what energizes the partners and keeps them committed to
the "marriage." The architects gather clues for the design of
the new facility from the accumulation of both the patrons'
and the library personnel's grumblings about how the current facilities no longer meet their functional needs and how
inconvenient or overcrowded the locations have become. The
architectural teams work hard to pull the partners' attention
away from what they have been doing and toward imagin-
ing what they could do in a new, bigger, and better building.
Working out the details of a joint library design is similar to
that of any library or large public-use facility—expectations
and price tags soar, then there is a reality check and the plans
become more modest due to lot size or budget constraints.
Just as in any library design, planning joint facilities takes
longer than expected and involves a vast amount of com-
promising before the final drawings are approved. Typically,
the designs of joint academic/public libraries have evolved
over a span of years with extensive conversations not only

with the library partners, but also with their constituencies to accurately assess their current and future needs (Leighton and Weber, 1999).

BEGINNING THE PROCESS

During the initial planning stages, the architects and designers first hear about the visible defects the library's staff and customers now face and expect to be remedied in a new facility. In the cases of the joint libraries that we studied, common justifications for the new libraries were the lack of flexibility in the layout, inadequate wiring to accommodate the array of patron and staff technology needs, poor lighting, scarcity of display areas, insufficient separation of children and adult areas, shortage of quiet areas, overcrowded shelving, reading areas with worn-out furniture and flooring, a variety of safety issues related to the age of the building, and, in some instances, even neighborhood deterioration. But it is usually the more costly but less visible defects that top administrators and funding authorities want to remedy in the design of a new joint library building: high energy consumption, skyrocketing costs for the maintenance and replacement of HVAC systems, elevators, roofs, and windows, plus inadequate plumbing and electrical systems. Administrators are sometimes forced to reconsider expansion plans for existing facilities after discovering that renovations would trigger substantially higher costs due to compliance requirements with the Americans with Disabilities Act, changes in fire and building codes, and new minimums for on-site parking, or, as in the Tomball county library situation, additional land acquisition and development costs for a second site more suitable for construction. All of these factors, along with the close proximity to another current or proposed library which serves overlapping segments of the same community, prompt decision makers to pause and look for other alternatives before asking for a bond referendum for capital funds for either a new stand-alone library or extensive renovations. The City of Virginia Beach and Tidewater Community College had initially planned to build new libraries across the street from each other before stepping back to investigate the advantages of building a single library both could use (Anderson Brulé 2005).

Typically the architectural firm is hired at this point in the planning and is responsible for starting the process of identifying, quantifying, and organizing the client's needs. The design is then developed based on those criteria. In the cases of the Dr. Martin Luther King, Jr. Library in San Jose and the Virginia Beach/Tidewater Community College library, the architectural firm of Anderson Brulé was hired to initiate the strategic and operational planning.

For the MLK library, the architects started with the premise that it was not "if" the merger would occur, but "how." The building was intended to be a seamless operation so that the users would never have to ask if they should be helped by a college librarian or a public librarian. The firm used a highly structured process which went through the issues layer by layer. They started with strategic planning, which established the vision and direction and then went to operational issues and finally developmental ones. They held over 160 meetings with the staff who would be working in the new San Jose library. Obviously the intense planning led to a smoother merger, but it also led to a smoother programming and design phase for the architects.

COST SAVINGS

The first assumption of why a joint library should be given a green light is that there will be significant cost savings because only one library will be built and maintained. For most joint libraries, the fiscal impact could more accurately be described as stretching taxpayer dollars by expanding the space, collections, services, and operating hours. Rather than reducing the overall costs, most joint libraries see their operating budgets go up because the square footage is significantly increased, additional personnel are hired to staff the larger facility, and the building receives heavier use than the replaced facilities, resulting in increases in the budget for collections and licensing fees, as well as additional security, housekeeping, utilities, maintenance, and supplies (Peterson 2005). Some cost savings are realized in new construction from the use of more innovative materials, the installation of more energy-efficient systems, and the avoidance of the costly repairs associated with maintaining an aged structure. The biggest cost saving for a joint library, however, is the land. Local government and college officials are easily persuaded to locate the joint public/academic libraries on college or university campuses because the academic institutions already own large tracts in anticipation of future expansion needs. Choosing campus locations frequently hastens the starting dates for joint library construction projects because there are not site locations to select, prolonged price negotiations with multiple landowners, nor land acquisition costs to fund. An additional financial advantage for joint libraries constructed on college/university campuses is that they have often been combined with other campus building projects, thus lowering the library's portion of the cost of road extensions, site preparation, installation of utility lines, parking lots, and so on. Library partners, construction costs, sizes, and architectural firms for some recent joint library facilities are listed in figure 5.1.

FIGURE 5.1
Joint Library Facilities

Library	Partners	Opening Date	Size (sq. ft.)	Architects	Cost
College Hill Library	City of Westminster Front Range Community College	Spring 1998	76,000	Bennett, Wagner, Grody	$10.3M
Alvin Sherman Library	Nova Southeastern University Broward County Public Library	Summer 2000	325,000	Smallwood, Reynolds, Stewart, Stewart	$43M
Dr. Martin Luther King, Jr. Library	San Jose Public Library San Jose State University	Summer 2003	475,000	Carrier Johnson Anderson Brulé	$177.5M
Lone Star College-CyFair Library	Lone Star College Harris County Public Library	Aug. 2003	78,500	Gensler CLR Cobourn, Linseisen & Ratcliff	$26.5 M
Lone Star College-Tomball Library	Lone Star College Harris County Public Library	Jan. 2005	72,000	PageSouther-landPage	$13.1 M
University Branch-Fort Bend County Library	Fort Bend County Public Library University of Houston-Sugar Land Wharton County Junior College	Nov. 2011	40,000	Bailey Architects	$6.2 M
Tidewater Community College Virginia Beach Campus Joint-Use Library	Tidewater Community College City of Virginia Beach	Spring 2013 (projected)	120,000	RRMM Architects Carrier Johnson Anderson Brulé	$53M

In joint libraries, the architectural wow factor and the more aesthetically pleasing features help capture broad public support. These extras or higher-quality features are more feasible because the combination of funding sources allow the projects more leverage to dream bigger and add the items that normally appear only on the design wish lists. Combining forces also often rewards joint libraries with more purchasing leeway. These partnerships may be exempted from some state and local purchasing restrictions and the typical low bid requirements for government construction projects. Jane Light, the director of the San Jose Public Library, mentions in her video that the San Jose Redevelopment Authority was designated as the purchasing agent for the MLK library instead of the public library or the university because the redevelopment agency already owned the proposed site and fortuitously did not have to be restricted to buying the state-mandated corrections agency furniture (Light 2008, video). Lyle Vance, former library manager of North Lake Community Library, states that partners often have different pails of money to work with, as was the case with the joint library at North Lake College. The college had construction funds that could easily be tapped, and the City of Irving had more funds readily available to spend on materials and furnishings (Vance, pers. comm.).

KEY ARCHITECTURAL FEATURES

In reviewing the descriptions of the joint public/academic libraries built in Fort Collins, Colorado; San Jose, Lafayette, and Lincoln, California; Cy-Fair, Fort Bend, and Tomball, Texas; and in the counties of Broward, Brevard, and Seminole, Florida, many similarities were found in the features of these new shared facilities. The common interior building attributes for these library projects included:

- collection spaces designed to create a more open feeling for the user
- circulation and information desk areas that were readily approachable and encouraged communication between users and staff
- expanded and more functional staff work areas
- optimization of natural lighting for both aesthetics and energy savings
- a mixture of individual, small group, and large group areas that incorporated access to electronic information resources and office productivity software
- upgraded hard-wired network to support high-speed Internet access and the rapidly evolving technology/digital media

- WiFi Internet access for patrons
- classrooms dedicated to information and computer literacy classes for children, adults, and college students
- media viewing and listening stations
- meeting areas that were flexible for use by internal and external groups and provided state-of-the-art presentation equipment along with convenient lighting and audio controls
- special use space such as tutoring, adult literacy areas, art displays, and local history rooms
- spaces that met the needs of previously underserved populations: teens, persons with disabilities, additional foreign language collections
- designated areas for community outreach, such as art displays, exhibit cases, local news postings, informational brochures for nonprofit/service organizations, and job placement assistance
- kitchens for public and staff use
- a wide variety of seating options for multigenerational use, including individual and group tables and chairs
- multiple quiet zones for extended reading or studying with colorful, comfortable, upholstered furniture
- an expanded number of computer stations, plus furniture and outlets that conveniently supported patron usage of personal technology
- shelving that enhanced browsing and encouraged use of the collection—display ends, tilted shelves that allowed easy removal of materials, a variety of sizes that adapted to the changing dimensions of materials in the collection, including compact shelving in academic libraries
- enclosed children's areas that were separate from the adult areas and encouraged exploration, celebrated the fun of reading, and accommodated families
- segregated spaces for noisier activities: teen rooms, children's story time, small group activities
- coffee and snack bars
- retail space for the Friends groups that help support the library
- flooring and walls that were durable and easily cleaned
- colorful signage
- equipment that increased operating efficiency and patron self-sufficiency—single-card systems for printing, checkouts, and room

reservations, self-checkout machines, RFID systems, inventory wands, and electronic information kiosks
- conveniently located, large, and accessible restrooms

The newest joint public/academic library that we studied is being built for Tidewater Community College and the City of Virginia Beach Public Library and is again incorporating many of these features. As the first joint library of its size in the region, the goal of the new Learning Resources Center is to be a center of academic distinction and sustainable integrity. The highly technical library will house spaces for computer labs, interactive labs, study spaces, display areas, meeting rooms, a café, staff work spaces, and designated areas for children and teens.

EXTERIOR FEATURES

The joint libraries shared many common exterior characteristics as well:

- a prominent or dramatic entry that was welcoming and not intimidating
- a building of significant size and shape to create a visible landmark for the area
- an attractive façade that not only matched the buildings in the adjoining area, but also captured a spirit of energy, community, and learning
- low-maintenance and sustainable materials that complemented the natural local setting
- extensive use of glass to maintain a connection with the outside setting and create an atmosphere of openness
- outdoor courtyard areas for programming/reading/socializing needs
- sheltered space at the entrance to serve as gathering spots for students and secure drop-off spots for children, persons with disabilities, buses, shuttles, and so on
- controlled entrances and exits that maintained the security of adjacent buildings and corridors when the library was part of a larger complex
- a well-lighted parking lot adjacent to the library with clear access paths to the library for both college and public patrons

The ease of access for patrons cannot be stressed enough. Plans for the LSC-CyFair Library were already under way as a community college library when the addition of Harris County, as the public library partner, was introduced. The original plans had the front portion of the library, the area that was closest to the parking lot, designated for student service activities such as admissions and registration. It was felt that this layout would not be accommodating to public library customers, so the library was reconfigured to put the college's student service functions in the back portion of the library. The result is still not a perfect plan. New students must walk through the library before they reach the admissions/registration area. Many of the parents and students stop and ask librarians questions related to registering for college courses before realizing that they are in the wrong area. To permanently remedy the confusing layout, the college has built a new separate registration building on campus that directly faces the parking lot.

The importance of having a joint library facility coordinate its appearance with the surrounding setting is highlighted in the University Branch Library. The agreement with the architectural firm, Bailey Architects, for the Fort Bend Library University Branch, which opened in the fall of 2011, was made with Fort Bend County, with the stipulation that after plans had been approved by the county, the University of Houston System would also have an opportunity to review and approve the plans. Since the library is located on the University of Houston System's Sugar Land campus, there was a deliberate attempt on the part of the architects to integrate the library building with the existing two buildings. The façade of the new library matches the other buildings and the furnishings are also coordinated. The architects felt that this similarity went a long way toward gaining the acceptance of the university personnel, even though this incorporation had not been mandated by the primary client, the county library.

According to Jeff Harris of RRMM Architects, the key to the design concept for the Tidewater Community College/Virginia Beach library is the connection between the organic forms of nature and the vibrancy of technology. The building's design (figure 5.2, rendering by RRMM) responds to its unique site on an abandoned agriculture field, where linear drainage ditches left a system of hedgerows. The building mimics this figuration with linear bands that run through the space and maximize the quiet areas of shadow and ambient light created by these garden hedges. In contrast, along the dramatic, curvilinear, south-facing wall is an interactive media wall that celebrates the flow of information, technology, and innovation (Jeff Harris, pers. comm.).

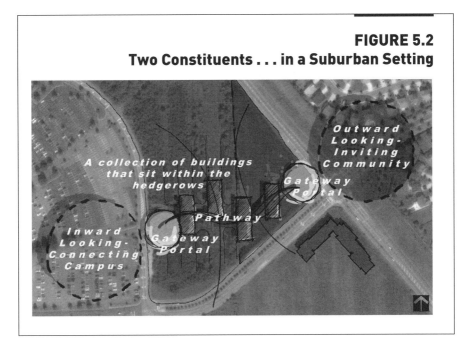

FIGURE 5.2
Two Constituents . . . in a Suburban Setting

INFRASTRUCTURE

The review of the descriptions of recent joint libraries also revealed numerous mechanical and maintenance elements that were less visible and less glamorous, but met critical functional needs in the new structures:

- up-to-date and robust network cabling
- wireless routers throughout the building
- zoned areas for heating and cooling to maintain a balanced and comfortable temperature throughout
- eco-sensitive fixtures that reduced energy and water consumption in toilets, faucets, sprinkler systems, and outdoor lighting
- adjustable lighting and sun control systems
- separate public and freight elevators in multistory structures
- enlarged freight docks and delivery-processing areas
- security-monitoring systems
- public address and messaging systems

- integrated technology such as electronic clocks, drop-down viewing screens, and adaptive software for children, persons with disabilities, and non-English speakers
- building materials that dampened noise and contributed to acoustic comfort
- lockable storage areas for extra furniture and equipment, custodial supplies, seasonal items, programming materials, and so on

LANDMARK QUALITIES

From the foregoing lengthy lists of features, it is evident that joint libraries have the luxury of erasing nondescript utilitarian pasts. In some cases, the joint libraries were deliberately built to become a significant landmark for the campus and an inspiring new piece of civic architecture for the community. In the particular case of the Dr. Martin Luther King, Jr. Library in San Jose, the library became the catalyst for the revitalization of economic development in the downtown area, and is said to have added millions to the economy in the first year. The newest trend is to build joint libraries as anchors in larger multiuse development projects such as the one that opened in September 2008 in the Miramar Town Center, a forty-acre residential, retail, government, and business office complex. This partnership between the City of Miramar, Broward College, the Broward Public Library, and the private Nova Southeastern University is known as the Miramar Branch Library and Education Center. The Broward County Branch Library occupies the first floor, Broward College's classrooms and offices are on the second floor, and Nova Southeastern offer its classes on the third floor of the building.

DEVELOPMENT TIME LINE

The design and construction time line for a joint library is not really different than that of any major library building project, except that the process can be lengthier and more emotional since there are more stakeholders involved. The architects have to be willing to work with representatives of all the partners so that the diverse current and long-term needs of the new occupants are considered, mutually agreed upon, and incorporated into the new structure. The project may be more complex for the architects and design teams because of the challenge of obtaining multiple layers of approvals for a joint library. If extensive modifications are required or financial situations change for one or more of the entities, the time line may be prolonged or the project may be delayed indefinitely while expectations are adjusted and wounds heal over. The initial discussions on the joint library between Mayor Susan Hammer and Robert Caret, the San Jose State University president, for example, started in 1997. Despite a number of floors being slashed from the original plans and the project almost being halted by a state budget analyst's report in 1999, the building was not derailed and it opened in 2003 (Breivik, Budd, and Woods 2005). On the other hand, the design process may move faster and more smoothly if the partners have had recent experiences in building other joint facilities. The architect for the University Branch of the Fort Bend County Library System commented in an interview for this book that the county library had recently built the Sienna Branch as a joint library with the Houston Community College District, which made it easier for the public library to articulate its needs during the assessment phase. Architects had a similar experience working with the clients on the CyFair joint library because it took place soon after the Harris County Public Library completed the Barbara Bush Branch, another large facility. The Tomball joint library took only two and half years from the initial announcement until move-in day because the two libraries had already developed their own plans for new facilities and the construction followed so closely on the heels of the joint facility that the same two partners had created in Cy-Fair.

In spite of the lengthy needs assessment process, intense bargaining among the partners, and repeated self-doubts among the planning participants if the projects really would or should happen, once the buildings open the vision of unity becomes a reality. The Miramar Library and Education Center was a nine-year project, and despite its ups and downs, as Robert E. Cannon, director of the Broward County Libraries Division, was quoted at the grand opening ceremony of this triple-partnership facility: "Everybody won" (Broward College 2008).

DESIGN REGRETS

Even though they received lavish praise for their inspiring edifices and cutting-edge technology, once the joint library buildings were opened and operating, numerous items were discovered that had been overlooked or awkwardly designed. At the San Jose library, they found that the loading dock was too far from the mailroom and the number of bathrooms was inadequate (Light 2008, video). At Tomball, the highly touted drive-up window initially lacked the necessary communication equipment to converse with the customers, and the staff was roasted by the blinding afternoon sun that struck the window until a customized awning (that did not obstruct the path for customers' vehicles) could be designed and installed.

Most of the joint libraries found their internal signage to be inadequate or confusing to the new mix of users. At Tomball the architects and designers painstakingly incorporated the different services and operating routines of the public and academic libraries into the design of the two-story building. It was not until the building opened for the spring semester that Victoria Waters, the Extended Learning Center manager, realized that close attention was not paid to the operating routines of the library building's third tenant, the college's heavily used testing center. Off by itself in a hidden corridor on the second floor of the library building, the testing center was in a beneficial location that helped create a quiet atmosphere for testing, but finding the entrance to the testing center was extraordinarily difficult for first-time students at the college. Prospective students would be sent by the admissions office to the library to take their college placement tests for English and math, and unless spotted by the staff, they would wander in circles because there was no visible signage indicating a testing center was in the building. Even after temporary signs were posted, most students had to be personally escorted to the testing center door by the library staff because the entrance was completely blocked from view by the walls surrounding the college's second-floor reserve desk.

A more significant detail that was overlooked was that the testing center, which needed to accommodate students taking distance learning courses and had full-time jobs, had earlier Saturday hours than the library, but it lacked a separate entrance. Because the testing center hours were already published in the college catalog and in the course syllabi, the hours could not be changed when the joint library opened during the middle of the academic year. Every weekend, signs and maps had to be posted on the front door of the library directing students to the second-floor entrance. The students would have to walk around the outside perimeter of the library building and then zigzag through two wings of the main campus building until they reached a security guard who would let them in through the back corridor. When the library staff entered the building on Saturday mornings, they would often find patrons who had slipped by the guard and had spent up to an hour on their own in the darkened stacks or impatiently pounding on the computers hoping they could make them turn on.

There were similar signage difficulties at the CyFair joint library, where the assessment center was located in the library as well. It was labeled "assessment center," but everyone called it the "testing center," creating lots of confusion.

Luckily, the director of the library and the director of the assessment center had time to coordinate hours before the library's official opening in August 2003. Another issue encountered in the Lone Star College-CyFair library was the lack of work space. The design plan completely overlooked the need for designated shelving for course reserves in the circulation desk area and provided little office space for library staff. The initial plan was for the eleven full-time librarians, the library director, and the manager of circulation to all have office space in the library, but, as it turned out, there are only eight offices in the library. The reason for the shortage was that five potential library offices were converted to quiet study rooms, the only ones in the library. The shortage turned out to be fortuitous because the librarians were given offices in the faculty suites, leading to more frequent collaboration and interaction between the librarians and the college's teaching faculty.

ADAPTABLE DESIGN NEEDS

Joint libraries often experience an influx of new users that change staffing patterns and may result in the need to reconfigure the layout and service point locations. As homeschooling has grown in popularity, libraries have become vital sources for curriculum materials and inviting gathering places for instruction for homeschooling groups. Having a way for homeschoolers and other customers to easily identify where and how they may schedule or reserve library classrooms and study rooms may become a new challenge. Libraries with a large number of meeting or study rooms will need user-friendly scheduling software to equitably and efficiently meet the growing requests from student groups, college committees and clubs, arts and craft groups, homeowner associations, scouts, senior groups, and book clubs. High demand for these rooms also means that library personnel need to be located nearby to lock and unlock doors, post reserved times, demonstrate how the equipment works, and reinforce the schedule if needed. Many new joint libraries have included separate teen rooms to encourage lifelong learning habits and give teens some creative space. Intentionally separated from the children's area and the adult areas, some libraries have found that the teen rooms offered too much isolation and required a more visible staff presence closer to the area.

An oft-repeated benefit of joint libraries is the expanded number of areas for computers, which means that reference desks, or at least roving reference personnel, need to be close by in order to help users find information online and monitor equipment problems. The more computers there are in the library, the more the reference staff has to multitask in order to handle the plethora of computer-related questions: how to print in color, find the full text of a journal article, adjust the volume on the headphones, save a file, update an online job application, delete the browser's history files, or view the electronic reserves for a psychology class. Librarians have also learned that large numbers of public-access computers mean that they have to take on a more active refereeing role to alleviate the friction that inevitably arises when different groups of stressed-out users are located side by side, especially during peak times for research papers, group projects, online job applications, tax deadlines, or final exams.

Having spaces that can easily be adapted for new or temporary uses gives joint libraries the flexibility to offer additional or enhanced services. At the Lone Star College-Tomball Community Library, the adult fiction, Spanish-language materials, and large-print items were shifted multiple times during the first few years due to an increase in demand and a realization that more open and well-lit locations for these materials would better serve the needs of the intended users. As word spread in the Spanish-speaking community that there were bilingual employees on the staff, there were numerous requests for story times and computer classes in Spanish. Several months after opening, the library began cosponsoring job search and resume-writing workshops with the state's workforce development agency to help the families from Louisiana that had been displaced by Hurricane Katrina. These workshops were continued on a regularly scheduled basis as the area unemployment rates rose. None of these new users or programs had been anticipated in the planning or design stages, but they could quickly be incorporated into the new building due to the built-in expansion space for shelving and the availability of multiple classroom spaces.

ADEQUATE PARKING

Convenient parking is the hardest and often the priciest feature to get right in a joint library. The majority of complaints received at joint libraries relate to the fact that the supply of parking spots does not meet the demand. The downside of opening a new joint library is that both the attractiveness of the new facility and the marketing of new library services and materials bring a rush of new and curious visitors which reinforces the perception that parking will always be a problem. Even after the newness wears off, community patrons are frustrated with having to compete with faculty and students for close-by parking spaces during peak class-time hours. Popular children's story times compound the problem because they are offered during the same heavily attended daytime hours as the college. Distant parking lots may be available but are real deterrents to frequent library use by older populations who have mobility and stamina issues and by parents with infants and rambunctious toddlers.

There are no cheap solutions to the parking issue. In areas where the land costs are high, large surface parking lots are expensive to construct and multistory parking garages are simply too unbearably costly to consider. Around the time many of the large joint libraries were being planned, an article was published in *Constructive Advice* that helps explain the parking dilemma:

> Surface parking costs about $1,500 per space and you can fit 100 to 120 spaces per acre, depending on how generously sized the spaces are. In contrast, the cost of a parking garage runs $8,500 to $10,500 per space and can go as high as $15,000 per space. If you decide to put in an underground garage, count on double to triple that amount. ("Parking Garages Come" 2001)

As one can see, the parking garage costs were high in 2001 and are even more prohibitive today. Garages are expensive for several reasons. More site preparation and excavation are required and more concrete and steel are used in the construction. Depending on what portion of the parking structure is open or underground, a ventilation system (that is constantly running) may also be required. In addition, elevators are needed in multilevel garages and can cost $100,000–150,000 per unit. The same article mentions that matching the exterior look of the garage to the library building's façade drives the price up even more. Although many realize that an adjacent garage would best meet the long-term parking needs of the library, parking garages are left out of joint library proposals because the price tag literally soars by millions. Getting taxpayer buy-in and bond approval to fund a multimillion-dollar library is tough, and adding millions more for parking accommodations makes it a much more difficult proposition to win, and therefore leads to the tendency to be overly optimistic that the minimum number of parking spots required by local building codes will be sufficient.

DESIGN DURABILITY

As a general rule of thumb, architects designing libraries try to project the space needs for the next twenty years. This is why it is imperative for the joint library partners to design their partnership before they design the building. Having a clear outline of each party's expectations for growth, changing demographics, funding, and long-term mission will lead to a facility that accommodates their vision and supports their partnership for years to come. The City of Virginia Beach/Tidewater Community College joint library feasibility study (Anderson Brulé 2005, 5) established the following broad criteria for the design of their lifelong learning center partnership:

- patron-, customer-, or user-centered goals
- universal access and universal design
- use of technology to deliver improved services
- equity in all respects for all involved
- seamless services perceived by users
- zoning of activities to meet diverse needs
- operational interaction to the extent achievable
- success of the system beyond this facility—other campuses and area libraries

Including a time-out for reflection after the initial design stages allows the partners in a joint facility to adequately assess their long-term goals and commitments. The partners in the University Branch of the Fort Bend library had initial meetings with the architects and intended to have a month's pause after completing the design process to confirm the agreement. Instead there was more than a yearlong hiatus. As the year progressed, one of the three partners, Wharton County Junior College, decided to decrease its level of funding for the construction of the project, but was still willing to contribute to the funding of the library.

After defining the big picture for the partnership, the design teams will then survey each partner to get a handle on the work flow and start conceptualizing the actual design. They will have questions similar to the ones that Philip Leighton and David Weber (1999, 55) presented in their book, *Planning Academic and Research Library Buildings:*

- How will the different collections be arranged?
- Will there be a need for controlled-access stacks?
- Are there different classification systems?
- Will the catalog be shared?
- How will the historic ownership of materials be handled?
- What is the financial arrangement for new materials, staffing, maintenance, and so on?
- Who will be in charge of building operations and maintenance?

- How will security be handled?
- Where will the processing of materials take place?
- Will there be one or two staffs?

Knowing up front that one of the entities will need additional space due to higher enrollments or population growth directly impacts the space configurations and allocations. Overbuilding a facility in anticipation of future growth usually does not happen because it unnecessarily raises the annual operating and staffing costs. If more floors or additions are to be phased in at later dates, the engineers need to know in advance in order to maximize the capacity of cooling and heating systems, provide adequate electrical power, and carefully select pipe locations, as well as reinforce the foundation for heavier loads.

FUTURE DESIGNS FOR JOINT LIBRARIES

There is already evidence that future joint libraries are on the threshold of dramatic change and will not look or operate the same as today's joint-use libraries. Joint libraries built in the past two decades offered more space, more high-tech features, more shelving capacity, and more staff, and thus required more funding. They were built during a period when government and higher education agencies had the revenues and reserves that allowed them to take risks and expand services and be a bit splashy. The prolonged downturn in the economy has changed the way all libraries are now viewed and how joint libraries will be utilized in the future. Trends spotted in more recent joint library endeavors are greater internal and external acceptance from the start, more intense scrutiny of operating costs, and a higher number of partners participating in the project. Over the years there has been a quiet shift in emphasis. Instead of being sold on their grandeur, there is a greater public acceptance of joint libraries simply because they are viewed as fiscally responsible projects that avoid duplication of taxpayer-funded services. Libraries of all types and sizes are facing severe budgets cuts, making joint libraries more palatable alternatives, especially to library employees, than closures, layoffs, or privatization. There are also a mounting number of incentive grants, legislation, and mandates on the state and local level for expanded inter-local partnerships. In California the list of government jointly funded projects of all types is rising because the state has clearly mandated that joint projects that share the costs, and especially those that find private support, take priority over other requests for construction funds (California State Library 2000). Because of the growing number of joint public facilities nationwide, joint libraries are no longer deemed as pioneering adventures. With decades of experience and dozens of locations throughout the state, joint libraries in Florida are no longer seen as the oddball arrangement, but rather the norm for providing library services to a wide number of users. In the Broward County Library System alone there are now six joint facilities in operation.

Newer joint libraries are emerging with more than two partners because the overlapping service boundaries among school districts, public library systems, community college districts, and state universities, and even private universities, are no longer sacrosanct. The North Natomas Library which opened in 2010, for example, serves three constituencies: the community, the high school, and the community college (CCS Partnerships 2011). As there is a growing awareness that the twentieth-century goal of library self-sufficiency is no longer affordable, the concept of joint library facilities is broadening beyond combinations of different types of libraries to include new types of partners: service agencies, recreational facilities, government offices, university consortia, shopping complexes, and residential developments, such as the Miramar Library and Education Center in Florida.

It was announced in 2010 that the new central library for the San Diego Public Library System would house a charter high school with 400 students for the San Diego Independent School District on its sixth and seventh floors. Earlier plans to include an elementary school, middle school, or regular high school were nixed because of stringent school earthquake standards. The fact that the construction of the showcase library began in August 2010 without details on how the charter school (exempt from earthquake standards) would operate alarmed many and led to a county grand jury investigation. Numerous design and security issues were detailed in the San Diego Grand Jury 2010/2011's report (2011, 3):

> The warmth, comfort, and facilities of the current downtown library attract indigents from the local streets. What are the plans to keep the students and the indigents separated at the new library school?

> Child predators will be able to mingle with the library patrons and be lost in the crowd. How will the students be protected?

> How will entrances and elevators be secured to ensure that only students, faculty, staff, and approved visitors are allowed to enter the school?

> Even under the best of circumstances, elevators and other areas of public buildings are subject to vandalism. With 400 students utilizing the library building daily, how will the facilities be protected?

William A. Kowba, the superintendent of the San Diego Unified School District, submitted his response to the grand jury's findings on July 11, 2011. Kowba outlined how the access and entry points would be designed to maximize the safety of the charter school students in the multiuse facility. The superintendent stated that the charter school would have a separate lobby and entrance from the library. For added security, two of the elevators would be solely for charter school use and would be programmed to go directly to the floors designated for the school (Kowba 2011, 6–7).

Building sites chosen for future joint libraries will be more closely analyzed due to sustainability initiatives to construct public use facilities in close proximity to public transportation, walking and bike trails, schools, and other needed services (New Schools/Better Neighborhoods 2003). Because of increased competition for construction dollars, joint libraries will be constructed where high usage will immediately occur rather than in outlying areas that expect gradual increases in usage as the population or enrollment expands. The trend toward controlled and compact growth and away from urban sprawl will also lead to more public acceptance of smaller renovated facilities over new construction.

Adapting to the widespread use of ever-changing technology will impact the design of forthcoming joint facilities not only because users now expect it, but because of its potential to hold down operating costs by reducing both the square footage and staff needed. Staffed service desks will shrink because intuitive user-interfaced technology will be everywhere, from multimedia electronic information kiosks with building maps and interactive navigation to overhead monitors that promote the library's or other community partner's programs. Libraries are already adopting Amazon-like data mining catalog systems that increase circulation and take over reader advisory duties by suggesting titles with similar themes or based on search terms' histories. The new systems also raise customer satisfaction because they direct users looking for high-demand items to materials that are readily available on the shelves. Libraries will soon join the "app brigade" as borrowers use their smart phones to handle all library transactions from payment of fines to study room reservations, database log-ins, copying, printing, and coffee bar purchases. Joint libraries, like other large libraries, are paying careful attention to ways to increase patron self-sufficiency and significantly reduce staffing costs with automated RFID check-in and book-sorting systems and more advanced and reliable self-checkout machines. The perpetually shrinking costs for new and more powerful technology make it affordable and convenient for the masses to use their own smart phones, tablets, laptops, and e-readers, which then lessen the demand on the library to provide the equipment and the in-house technical support needed to access electronic information. There are also indications that the demand for physical gathering spaces in the library will eventually diminish as more and more users embrace social networks with integrated, high-resolution video capabilities offering virtual face-to-face interactions.

The footprint of future joint libraries will be more compact, as mentioned above, due to the increased use of technology, but also due to the adoption of the most cost-effective management models, leading to further reductions in the amount of staff office space needed. Dual management systems have proven that they are viable models at the College Hill Library in Fort Collins, the Lone Star College-Tomball Community Library, and the Dr. Martin Luther King, Jr. Library in San Jose. However, single-management operating models are still preferred in the literature and deemed more likely predictors for success (Haycock 2006). In the age of shrinking budgetary support and shifting expectations, every position and budget item will have to be justified. Dual management systems could be perceived as another unaffordable luxury when the space requirements and true overhead costs for duplicated efforts for administration, insurance, payroll, training, recruiting, purchasing, collection development, and so on are factored in. Cococino Community College, for example, closed its library in 2010 due to severe budget cuts and entered into what it referred to as an "innovative alliance" with Northern Arizona University's Cline Library to provide library services for its students (Cococino Community College 2010). The new alliance calls for the community college to reimburse the university based on tracked usage of the library resources by the community college students and eliminates any duplication of staff or services.

Universities are also investigating new vigorous alliances for sharing library resources. According to a press release from the Cornell University Library (2011), the 2CUL Project with Columbia University will create a new nonprofit entity for what James Neal, vice president for information services and university librarian at Columbia University, described as a "radical form of collaboration" for collection development, digital access, and improved efficiency. Many other universities and public library districts are consolidating their own libraries and reducing their acquisition of new materials. Although Cornell and Columbia are in the vanguard, libraries across the county are building stronger regional library partnerships with a greater reliance on reciprocal borrowing, consortium purchases of electronic resources, and spending larger portions of their collection development funds on rapid, reliable delivery services. These new alliances fulfill both the users' needs of having access to a greater number of resources and the libraries' needs to lower their costs. These types of alliances also have the distinct advantage of avoiding the hassles of cohabitation, the costs of relocations, and the loss of brand identity associated with sharing the same physical space. Whatever form they take, joint libraries will continue to represent how unifying efforts can help libraries adapt to the demographic, fiscal, technological, and environmental changes in their surroundings.

SIX

LEGAL CONSIDERATIONS

*A compromise is the art of dividing a cake in such a
way that everyone believes he has the biggest piece.*

—Ludwig Erhard, German economist
and politician (1897–1977)

Dealing with the legal aspects of a joint library is a complex
endeavor. The process of creating a joint library requires
approval from different governing agencies, boards, and
funding sources—each with its own cadre of cautious and
protective legal experts. There are many similarities in language and topics covered in the formal agreements that bind
the partners together, but as stated in the research report
by the Center for Cities and Schools at the University of
California-Berkeley: "Overall, we find that joint use partnerships are locally driven, and vary significantly in how they
are structured and implemented from place to place" (Center
for Cities and Schools 2010, 2).

Before the actual agreement for a joint library can be
drafted, there are often preliminary approvals or reviews
that need to be sought from various state, federal, and local
regulating bodies. Because a joint agreement needs to spell
out the long-term fiscal commitments and operational details
for all parties, one can understand why many months, and
sometimes years, pass between the time the initial plan is
announced and the formal operating agreement is finalized.

Formal legal documents are used by the entities to protect the interest of all parties, but just as important, they establish the collaborative foundation and mutually beneficial policies and practices that will fund and support the smooth operation of the joint library. There are multiple goals for the negotiations that precede the signing of the agreement: these include constructing the framework for the operation of the library so it may function without unneeded obstacles, disputes, or uncertainty; performing due diligence and establishing the legal owner of the facility, the collections, the furniture, and the equipment; and last, clearly articulating the role and responsibilities of each of the library partners using and/or staffing the facility. Since leadership personnel and institutional perspectives may dramatically change—even in the few short years between the initial informal discussions about the possibility of a joint library and the day the facility actually opens—it is imperative that the full scope of the decisions reached in the negotiation are in writing. The most secure way to guarantee the partnership into the future and avoid litigation and continuous internal disagreements is to take the time to develop a well-written and detailed—but not overly restrictive—binding contract.

WRITTEN AGREEMENT

The agencies wanting to pursue joint library partnerships will, in many cases, need to submit a letter of intent, or memorandum of understanding, with broad details on the proposal to their boards, city councils, county commissioners, state agencies on higher education, and so on to receive formal permission to start the process of negotiations and announce the proposal to the public. After acceptance of the letter of intent, the next steps are the designation of who will officially be authorized to participate in the development of the agreement, assembling the designees together to start the negotiations, and forming subcommittees to gather the additional information that will be needed.

The typical components found in the formal agreement for a joint library include:

- background information on the project, along with the mission and goals for the library
- a description of the building's size, capacity, and features
- initial term period
- funding and payment details for the construction or anticipated renovations

- ownership of the building, materials, and equipment
- ongoing responsibilities for maintenance and repairs
- day-to-day management, supervision, staffing, and reporting requirements and operating hours
- insurance and liability coverage
- allocation formulas and methodologies for distributing operating costs
- payment schedules
- a plan for conflict resolution
- renewal and term modification options
- steps required for dissolution or early termination

(Note: Sample agreements are included in the appendixes, and the URLs for several others are noted in the "References" list.)

SHARED EXPECTATIONS

Typically, the key players in the negotiations meet, select additional members of the subcommittees, and work out an initial time line. The next step, and often the easiest to achieve, is to formulate a statement of how the joint library will be mutually beneficial, along with a mission statement and a description of the shared goals. Agreeing on the common vision and the nature and scope of the project up front helps to create an atmosphere that promotes continued collaboration and compromise—essential ingredients for working out the details on how the joint library will actually be run.

Facility Description and Ownership

Describing the building, its location, size, major functions, traditional as well as bold new features and services, plus a complete list of all the intended occupants (other departments, agencies, etc.) is the next portion of the agreement that is usually readily agreed upon, especially if the architects or other consultants facilitate these meetings. The description of the facility does not cover explicit information on the layout because the design is still a work in progress. Having some idea of the general layout, however, lets the partners start to visualize what departments or what portions of the building it makes sense to completely share and what unique spaces need to be retained. Who owns, pays for, and has final decision-making authority concerning the building, the land, the parking lots, the collections, the furnishings, and the equipment all need to be addressed in the agreement.

At this point there may be an unexpected power struggle over the naming or phrasing of the name of a joint facility. It might be a sensitive issue, but it should not be avoided or assumed that it will become less sensitive as time goes on. It is best to have the name settled up front and in writing before opening day. Finding an acceptable name that is recognizable by all segments of users, equally identifies the participating partners, is easily repeated by the staff, and still fits on the side of building, name tags, property stamps, brochures, web pages, and business cards can be touchy to negotiate. The employees of the Tomball joint public/academic library patiently waited for four years for name tags and business cards while the college district's public relations department took on the challenge of selecting a name and specifying the size and placement of logos that appeased all parties. Some joint libraries have asked their constituencies to weigh in on possible names for the new facility as a marketing strategy to keep the interest high in the progress for the joint library, but even in these situations not everyone develops the same fondness for the new name.

Operational Responsibilities and Staffing

The majority of the negotiations, and thus the core of the document, focuses on the gritty details of management and operational responsibilities, staffing, and the allocation of costs and payments. At this point in the negotiations, the participants start to recognize the complexity and uniqueness of each entity and, if they have not already done so, will hire consultants to help mediate the tensions and keep the project on track. The subcommittee members charged with formulating drafts of the agreement will often feel bombarded by their own constituencies with information about the inherent differences between the libraries and their internal preferences. Each side can be equally persuasive in their justifications for maintaining current policies and long-term operating practices. Even though it can be a rough and unwieldy process, delineating the operating details and formalizing them in the agreement is critical for the success of the project because it diminishes the number of internal turf battles that could subsequently harm the future functioning of a joint library facility or create permanent barriers among its employees.

The expectation for many joint libraries is that the building will be open for a greater number of hours than what is currently offered. Establishing the hours of operation for a joint public/academic library requires more compromises than most people expect. Academic libraries typically open earlier in the day and stay open later at night and on the weekends. Public libraries typically are open only for a few nights per week. Academic libraries also have periods during winter and spring break when they may shut down completely or have reduced hours. Public libraries, on the other hand, operate the same hours each week, except for major holidays. It is important to document in the agreement the mutually agreed upon weekly hours of operation and how the holiday schedule will be determined.

Designating which partner or partners will run the library facility and clearly stating how the management responsibilities are to be divided will enable the library to function on a day-to-day basis with minimal chaos or later intervention by higher authorities. The libraries adopting an integrated model with a single management system will obviously not have as lengthy a description of responsibilities as those adopting dual or hybrid management models. As noted in the California State University review of the proposed San Jose joint library: "almost all involve one public entity contracting with another to operate the library. This is a much less problematic arrangement because the library building and land are owned by one entity and the other entity simply contracts for space and operating personnel. Such an arrangement can easily be disentangled if cost and operational disagreements arise" (Eanes 2010, 62). Whichever operating model is chosen, the reporting chain of command needs to be spelled out. If a new governing body is to oversee the library, the agreement should entail details of its makeup and frequency of meetings. Provisions for scheduled reporting and auditing should be plainly stated, as well as who is responsible for submitting and approving annual budgets. The agreement should specify which entity's rules will govern purchasing activities and also the levels of approvals needed for high-cost expenditures. To aid the smooth day-to-day operation, the partners may even find it valuable to spell out the responsibility and level of technical support that will be provided for the library's automation system, e-mail, staff and public access computers, and telephones.

Once the decision on management of the facility is made, a general description of the categories of users the joint library is expected to serve (community patrons, faculty, students, and other consortia members) and the levels of service to be offered should be developed. Which party or parties are responsible for circulation, reference, acquisitions, cataloging, interlibrary loan, courier delivery, library instruction, children's programming, and community outreach services needs to be established. Again, this section is short if all of the services are merged and one entity is in charge. More details are needed if separate staffs are elected, specific positions are funded by a particular entity, or selected services are to be contracted out to a third party (book jobbers, for example). This portion of the agreement will also identify particular collections or floors that will have restricted rather than universal usage.

Many times a joint library replaces two existing libraries, which means there needs to be a determination of how the materials each partner brings to the shared facility are organized and managed. Deciding in advance if the materials are to be fully physically integrated, partially commingled, or each partner will house and maintain its own collections assists in the determination of space allocations, layouts, and staffing. If the total collection or selected portions are integrated, there will also need to be a decision on whether the Dewey Decimal or Library of Congress classification system is to be used and how the cost of conversion will be handled. If the two libraries use different automation systems, an analysis needs to be conducted to determine which current or new system will best meet the needs of both partners and how such a migration will occur. The agreement should be stated in such a way that it is flexible enough to allow for adjustments in collection development and automation decisions because attitudes, usage patterns, and technology will undoubtedly change in the new facility.

Maintaining a secure, clean, and attractive facility is important to all of the joint partners and is critical for continued support from the various groups of customers using the shared facility. When sharing physical space, it is imperative that the supervisors and managers in the building know, for instance, who is responsible for providing custodial services, elevator and air conditioning repairs, and who is authorized to replace or repair computers and other equipment. Besides routine maintenance and repairs, the document should also address how and when additional capital improvements, such as additional parking, will be authorized, scheduled for construction, and paid for.

Joint libraries have developed a variety of staffing options that best fit their shared facilities. At the Harris County Public Library/Lone Star College-CyFair Library, for example, it was determined that Lone Star College, as the owner of the building, would also have the responsibility of supervising and paying all of the library employees, with the county contributing funds for a certain specified number or portion of other positions. The CyFair agreement (see appendix A for a copy) also stipulates that the hiring process include representatives of both library partners. Looking at a different model, the joint libraries located on the north and south campuses of Broward College are operated by the Broward County Library System and all of the employees are hired by the public library. Other joint libraries have dual employers, with each partner retaining its own management structures and supervisory responsibilities, such as the Dr. Martin Luther King, Jr. Library shared by San Jose Public Library and San Jose State University, the Lone Star College-Tomball Community Library shared with Harris County Public Library, and the College Hill Library, shared by Front Range Community College and the City of Westminster, Colorado. Whichever staffing model is selected, mutual responsibilities for interview committees, training, supervision, and evaluations should be explained in the agreement.

Insurance and Liability

The unexpected does happen—even in libraries. The agreement needs to cover the indemnity responsibilities of each party. Partners in shared facilities also need to protect themselves with adequate insurance coverage for buildings and collections due to vandalism, fires, floods, and so on. If materials and equipment are separately owned, there will also need to be a procedure for verifying that each party has its own policy and adequate coverage for its portion of the facility.

Cost and Revenue Allocations

The amount each partner is expected to contribute for construction, furnishings, start-up costs, and opening day collection expenditures needs to be put in writing as well as the formula for expenses that each partner will bear on an annual basis. How much each partner contributes for ongoing operating costs for utilities, maintenance, security, and vendor services in some cases is based on the square footage allocated to each partner. But others, such as the Alvin Sherman Library shared by Nova Southeastern University and the Broward County Library System, rely more heavily on usage formulas for dividing the annual costs. Formulas for personnel costs depend on the level of consolidation and the number of hiring authorities in the facility. The payment schedule for annual costs needs to take into consideration the variances in fiscal years of each partner. To avoid disputes such as the one that occurred between Nova Southeastern University and Broward County over the usage calculations for the Alvin Sherman Library, the agreements should also incorporate the details on the methodology used for determining usage levels and allow a reasonable time to notify the other partner of an expected cost increase. Another issue that should not be avoided is how the partnership may be modified if the fiscal support for one or all of the entities dramatically changes, which would require a reduction in agreed-upon staffing levels or hours of operation.

In addition to tackling the distribution of costs and expenditures, the formal agreement should also clarify what happens to the fees and revenues collected for lost or overdue items, space rentals, copying and printing, book sales, and food and beverage operations. If these funds are retained by the library, how they are allocated among the partners and for what purposes they may be used should be outlined. At Lone Star College-Tomball Community Library, creating a joint library changed the standard procedure which had previously required the library to deposit all fees collected into the parent institution's general fund. As part of the joint library memorandum of agreement, the fees collected at Tomball were deposited into a library account and allocated between the public library and the college library based on past circulation statistics for fees and lost items. Being able to retain the "fee" money at the library fortified the partnership because the funds were used for professional development, guest speakers for public programs, as well as joint purchases of expensive reference sets or new equipment, such as specialized early literacy computers for the children's department.

Conflict Resolution

The website for the collaborative New Schools/Better Neighborhoods initiative in California points out that for any joint endeavor it is imperative that a method for dealing with unresolved conflicts be stipulated in the agreements (New Schools/Better Neighborhoods 2003). Having a tiered mechanism in place to handle library conflicts that are not resolved satisfactorily at the building management level reinforces the idea that upper management will remain visibly supportive and will do whatever it takes to sustain the partnership. At Lone Star College-Tomball Community Library, the two codirectors met weekly to share plans and resolve issues. During the first year or so they also met regularly with an executive committee composed of the next higher level representatives from each entity for approval for large-ticket items and guidance on strategic planning. Any issues that could not be resolved by the executive committee were to be bumped up to the college president and the county commissioner—an option that never had to be utilized.

Renewal and Termination Terms

Joint libraries are foreseen as long-range commitments, and some even anticipate lasting into perpetuity. Despite the partners' optimism and determination to collaborate at the time of conception, joint library agreements need to protect the substantial monetary investments of all parties by including specific details on when and for how long the agreement may be renewed and when and how it can be dissolved. The initial Memorandum of Understanding between Richmond County and the Rappahannock Community College in Warsaw, Virginia, for a joint library was for four years (Richmond County Public Library 1998). In contrast, the three-party agreement for the shared library at Twelve Bridges in Lincoln, California, has an initial term of a "minimum of 55 years" (City of Lincoln et al. 2003, section 2.1). On the other hand, some joint libraries might be established as temporary solutions and have a mutually accepted termination date because the space is expected to be needed by the host partner for future growth or one of the entities anticipates greater availability of its own capital funds in the future. Ending a joint library arrangement causes turmoil. Some joint libraries ended their partnership because they found the agreement too confining, they were disappointed that the expected cost savings did not occur, or the usage was lower than anticipated (Bundy 2003). Others no longer had the funding to cover the annual increases in expenses or wanted to develop other new alliances with other partners, as in the case of the Azalea Library in St. Petersburg, Florida (Bauer 2006). Whatever the reasons for the breakup, clear designations of ownership of materials and equipment explicated in the agreement promote quiet and orderly departures. Notification requirements for dissolution give each partner sufficient time to adjust its budgets, develop a moving-out schedule, and plan its new solo operations or partnerships plus it avoids the legal costs and public relations messes that surround abrupt evictions.

Many library personnel involved in the process of developing joint libraries would agree with Cathy Park, director of the Harris County Public Library, who participated in the creation of three joint libraries that opened in a span of three years, that the process is not pretty and can be filled with "agony" (Park, Murray, and Campa, 2007, PowerPoint slide 1). Yet many joint library administrators have publicly stated how essential it was to have such a road map and something official they could rely on when issues came up. Even in times of conflict, the document also acts as a gentle reminder of what they have in common with their partners and what the original aspirations were for the joint library. The formal agreement should not just get the joint library launched, but it should also create a sound and well-thought-out platform for continued smooth operations. The agreement becomes a tool that the library management can use to understand and respect the distinctions and boundaries established by each partner and keep the focus on the many opportunities for collaboration. The formal signed agreement is also a symbolic peace agreement that indicates to employees of every rank that the battles (the big ones, at least) are over, and they need to embrace the changes and compromises that were negotiated and realign their own personal goals to match the shared goals. A joint library agreement functions as a protective shield for each entity, but it also ensures that the concept of the new library is not marred in transit and can survive in the new environment, under both current and future leadership, and successfully serve the former and potentially new customers of all of the partners.

Additional Areas of Legal Concern

Not everything that needs legal review or approval will become part of the formal agreement or can be anticipated before the joint library begins operations. There are several known issues that joint libraries encounter that have legal implications. These management types of issues may be best ironed out after a few months of real experience in the new library setting and simply require standardization of policies and procedures or the investigation of best practices adopted at similar joint libraries. Some of the dilemmas that joint libraries have had to face and then negotiate satisfactory compromises revolve around conflicting policies on Internet filtering, copyright compliance, computer usage violations, protecting the privacy of student records, unaccompanied minors, meeting room use, handling challenged materials, penalties for theft or loss of materials, removal of unruly patrons, and even parking lot disputes. Maintaining a respectful attitude and open dialogue helps resolve these sticky legal issues and prevents knee-jerk reactions that the staff later cannot realistically implement. In most cases, dramatic changes are not required. Instead there needs to be an adjustment or clarification of current policies so consistent levels of service are provided to all library users. To give just one example, public libraries and college libraries vary in their policies, procedures, and rates for outside use of their facilities. To avoid complaints of discrimination or unfair treatment, joint libraries need to establish policies defining the meeting spaces that may be utilized, the types of permitted users, the hours of use, how the spaces are reserved, the amount of fees (if any) for setting up the room, security, equipment, housekeeping, and food service.

Reality Check

As witnessed over the past several years, operating budgets for libraries of every type and size are being reduced. As a result, one would expect that more attention will be paid in the future to those portions of joint library agreements related to staffing levels, renewal terms, how costs are allocated over the term of the partnership, and what, if anything could change the allocation formula. There have been increasing concerns not only about the cost-effectiveness of building joint use libraries, but also the long-term commitment to operate and maintain these facilities. Because of tougher budgetary scrutiny, future joint library agreements will have more accountability verbiage and more explicit expectations for costs savings. As the KPMG consultants warned in their report on shared service facilities in the United Kingdom, the parties will also want the agreement to have stronger penalties for nonperformance in case one of the participants wants to back out of the arrangement or reduce their contribution prematurely (KPMG 2006, 25–26).

Alan Bundy and Larry Amey (2006) make the case that joint libraries also need to have an evaluation plan in place that frequently measures the performance of the joint library and presents a true picture of how the library is achieving the stated goals of all the partners. Although it might be difficult to develop a consensus on evaluation methods and implement and maintain the plan on a regular cycle, embracing a routine of critical analysis may have long-term benefits in nurturing collaboration among administrators and employees and prevent an internal crisis that could lead to the dismantling of the partnership.

SEVEN

COLLECTION DEVELOPMENT

A library is a growing organism.
—Shiyali Ramamrita Ranganathan

One of the reasons given for a joint library is greater access to materials. Marie sums it up as "library planners involved in developing these libraries discovered with their combined financial resources, these institutions could provide users with larger, more attractive facilities and more extensive, higher-quality collections than anyone could by itself" (Marie 2007, 23). In a previous chapter we discussed the design of facilities, and we will now turn to how these "extensive higher-quality collections" are attained.

The concern for the library is how to most efficiently achieve the best collection. Eliminating duplication is frequently the most important result of a joint library. Librarians should consider the particular audiences for their collections and review their goals and collection development statements and policies. Although each partner library will retain its own collection goals, each will also need to get a sense of the newly shared goals and how the areas complement and enhance each other. There will need to be a section of the joint agreement specifically devoted to collection development and management. This section should cover such points as the ongoing commitment generally and responsibilities for maintaining periodicals, databases, and reference collections. It needs to be flexible enough to change as demands or means of access change and budgets fluctuate.

COMMUNICATION

As in all areas of a joint library, communication between the two entities is critical for collection development. There will need to be a good working relationship. The Dr. Martin Luther King, Jr. Library in San Jose developed a formal committee to work out the coordination between the collections. This structure involved several librarians, which may not be as necessary for smaller libraries. By contrast, at Lone Star College-CyFair library, initially there was only one collection development librarian who coordinated with the adult specialist at the Harris County Public Library. The two met in person on occasion, but communicated primarily by telephone or e-mail. HCPL developed the children's and teen areas entirely on its own.

The structure of book ordering may vary widely, as some public libraries are developing a more centralized ordering system, particularly in large multi-branch districts. Academic libraries are more likely to have subject librarians who will be more involved in collecting for their particular area. Each partner may have contracts in place with different vendors and rely on its vendors for different levels of service, from basic order fulfillment to full-service, shelf-ready materials. At HCPL, the ordering is largely centralized, with options for individual branches to fill in collection gaps with a small portion of the collection development funds. For new branches, there is a heavy reliance on Brodart as a vendor to develop "an opening day" collection from a profile based on similar existing branches.

Before opening the library, the two organizations should compare collections, whether existing or new. Some libraries, such as the MLK library, developed an extensive structure for determining overlap among the two collections. The collection management/technical services sub-team had ten members and met every two weeks for nearly two years before the library opened (Kauppila, Belanger, and Rosenblum 2007, 35).

Since the independent goals of academic and public libraries are usually different, there may not initially be much overlap. Most of the libraries we surveyed which had existing collections did not report a high level of duplication. Of course, duplication of materials is not necessarily a problem, particularly for circulating materials, as there is now a larger pool of library borrowers as well. However, since the goal of the merger is to provide both sets of patrons access to a wider range of materials, duplication should be avoided when possible to allow each entity to purchase as many unique items as possible. This is particularly important for reference materials and periodicals.

REFERENCE AND PERIODICALS

Agreements should be reached on which periodicals and reference materials to keep, particularly for materials that were duplicated. The MLK library has a formal procedure listed in its Cooperation in Periodicals Subscription policy. Since budgets may change, there needs to be flexibility in these agreements. One of the other libraries we surveyed was given funding from the partner library to maintain the collection for both partners. This agreement was reviewed periodically, which meant that the agreement to fund the collection could change within a year's time.

The savings on periodicals was a great boon to the opening of the LSC-CyFair library of the Harris County Public Library. The budget from the community college district was a relatively small $100,000 in 2002. Typically the college had in its collection a selection of popular periodicals on current issues, such as *Time* and *Newsweek*, as well as the local newspaper. Since those were being subscribed to by the public partner, the college could focus on more scholarly periodicals. Both sides had made the decision to retain only current periodicals, with all retrospective issues only available online through databases.

Online Periodicals and Databases

As more periodicals, books, and videos become available electronically, online access of these materials must be taken into consideration. Are patrons of each institution allowed to use databases only while in the library or may they also use them off-site? The expansion in levels of usage may affect licensing fees for online resources since database pricing structures vary—with some based on the number of simultaneous users, and others based on the size of the population served, the number of library cardholders, or in the academic setting, on the number of FTEs (full-time equivalent students). Moreover, agreements that specify that a respective institution would continue certain resources may be affected by a switch to online-only access.

There may be databases which each institution has a subscription to but which would require different authentication. For example, on the Lone Star College website, there are two listings for databases which both the college system and the public library have access to, since they must be verified by different proxy servers for off-site usage. Other databases may have different holdings for different subscriptions, such as netLibrary. Patrons may easily access items on-site and assume they have access to the entire collection off-site, yet are surprised to discover that they are restricted from viewing the full text remotely. The ability of all patrons to access all databases on-site only is fairly common. In contrast, however, patrons visiting the University Branch of the Fort Bend library will only have on-site direct access to the public library databases. Thus, in order to use the university's databases, University of Houston students will have to use the remote authentication as they would when they are not on campus.

CLASSIFICATION

The arrangement of the circulating nonfiction section is frequently one area of debate. Should materials be interfiled and thus employ one set of call numbers? The MLK library employs the Library of Congress (LC) system for the joint reference collection and uses both Dewey and Library of Congress for the circulating collection, as does the College Hill Library, the joint library partnered by Westminster Public Library and Front Range Community College, and the Alvin Sherman Library at Nova Southeastern University. The Lone Star College-Tomball Community Library has two sets of collections for both public and college, whereas the Lone Star College-CyFair library is totally interfiled using the Dewey system.

The hurdle for public libraries to embrace LC entirely frequently seems insurmountable. However, given the lack of specificity in cataloging using Dewey (and truncating numbers to only 1 or 2 digits past the decimal point, as is frequently done in public libraries), there may be issues with college and university collections which have large numbers of materials under one call number. The ability to distinguish subheadings may be lost or items which would be grouped together under LC may be separated by Dewey, leading some patrons to miss pertinent items. Under the shortened Dewey, for example, 813.52 is the call number for American literature from 1900 to 1945 and includes a great many authors. Since the titles are further categorized by the author of the work, books about the same author may not be next to each other. Since this can be a large collection, the gaps between titles could be a matter of shelves. For the LSC-CyFair collection, this is definitely one drawback. The call number 813.52 covers eight shelves. If a patron looks up the call number and goes to the shelf to find a specific item he should be successful, but it does hinder the patron who browses the shelves for similar items or biographical information about the writer. Students, particularly students new to the academic life, may not realize that there are more materials nearby.

According to Jay Shorten, OCLC reports that 25 percent of academic libraries use Dewey, while 95 percent of public and school libraries do. LC was adopted by large numbers of academic libraries due to its specificity and shorter numbers. From these statistics, we can conclude that almost no public libraries would employ LC.

Does the faculty of the institution expect the collection to be arranged by LC? Is there an expectation that students should know something of LC, either in the case of community college students who may be transferring to larger institutions or students who may be going on to graduate school? Is the library classification system still an issue in the days when students rely more and more on online resources? Are there library supporters among the faculty who use the library heavily for their own research and would find it difficult to adapt to change? These are some of the issues to take under consideration.

If there are existing collections, there is the consideration of the cost of a retrospective conversion. As mentioned, Front Range decided to keep circulating collections separate, but converted the public library reference collection to LC to keep it all in one location (Sullivan et al. 2006, 573). This decision was made in part due to the cost. The decision to merge the reference collection at the MLK library was based on the determination that there was little overlap between the two reference collections (Kauppila, Belanger, and Rosenblum 2007, 262).

If the two collections are not interfiled and are arranged by two sets of call numbers, it could be more time-consuming for the patrons since they may have to look in two sections. With separately arranged collections, the library is then committed to a perpetual sense of two collections, which may carry over in attitudes about the library and divided territories among both patrons and staff. There may also be tendencies to duplicate items for each area, thereby defeating one of the goals of the joint library: the cost efficiency.

Public patrons may feel that the academic section is intended for students and may be reluctant to use it. "Although in most UK joint use libraries the school and public stock is intershelved, at Haywood City Learning Centre in Stoke-on-Trent, until recently, the public and school resources were separated. This meant that half of the library, the "school side," was seen as a "no go area" by members of the public" (McNicol 2006, 526). Although the library mentioned is a public/school library, the same feeling may exist in any setting.

ACCESSIBILITY

Another faculty concern is the loss of access to college materials, both in the sense of theft and materials simply checked out to public patrons. The MLK library anticipated some problems. A faculty member at San Jose State University "envisioned scenarios in which tenth graders checked out stacks of books in an effort to beef up the bibliographies of their required papers in English class" (Guernsey 1998, A25). The solution that the library developed is that "the Operating Agreement states that should problems arise regarding student access to books necessary for their classes, the city is obligated to help the university find a solution, including the possibility of restricting access to certain materials. Additionally, faculty members and students will be able to recall any books checked out by other library members" (Kauppila and Russell 2003, 263). Typically, academic libraries have more pressure to bring to bear on patrons with overdue or recalled materials since students cannot get their diplomas, register for another semester, or check out additional materials if they have overdue items; while public libraries may block users' library cards, they have fewer (and often more lenient) methods to ensure materials are returned promptly.

Libraries may have special collections reserved for their particular patrons. Many academic libraries have materials "on reserve" for students, which may contain items pulled from the collection, but intended for students to use with a shorter checkout time, such as two hours. At the LSC-CyFair library, the public library's administrators did not want public library materials ending up on the reserve shelves for long periods. It was decided that any materials intended for course reserves or "faculty only" use had to be purchased with college funds. There are some difficulties in adhering to this policy since the library collection is totally interfiled. Faculty would often see items in the library catalog that they wanted to use throughout the semester for their courses, without knowing which partner was the owner of the material, and would then be disappointed they could not place the items on reserve for their students.

Borrowing privileges may also be a concern to faculty. Many faculty are accustomed to longer checkout times and no fines for overdue items. There may need to be a special borrower type for faculty, which may be resented by those on the public library side. The compromise reached for the Lone Star College system is that the faculty and staff are not charged overdue fines for materials checked out at an LSC library, but the materials are checked out for the normal loan period. This concern with loan periods seems particularly relevant since patrons can see when items are due on the online catalog. Public patrons might resent not having items available to them, without realizing that the materials are funded by the academic partner.

The age of library items may also come into consideration. Academic libraries may want to retain older resources for their historic and retrospective values or to show students how viewpoints and acceptable language have changed over time. Public libraries, because of the heavy focus on circulation counts, are more apt to want to have only the most current information on the shelves. Harris County Public Library, the partner of Lone Star College for the LSC-Tomball and LSC-CyFair libraries, has a strict collection development policy of not adding materials older than two years. Under these guidelines, materials with older publication dates that needed to be purchased to support the curriculum at CyFair were not handled through the routine channels at HCPL, but instead were sent to the college district's central technical services office for processing and cataloging. This same concern about the age of the collection applies to weeding materials.

JOINT COLLECTION BENEFITS

There are benefits to having a joint collection that may not be obvious at first. Frequently the assumption is that the public will get access to college materials without much consideration to the benefits for college students. For students who are learning English as a second language, public library materials may provide them with a wider range of reading materials on a more accessible level. Materials purchased for teens, including nonfiction items such as biographies or computing, because they are written at a young adult level, may be appropriate for those still grappling with the English language.

The same may be true for students in transitional or development-level classes in the community college. The LSC-CyFair library developed a list of popular fiction in the library that would be of interest to students in transitional English classes. Such a list encourages students to find materials that they would enjoy reading (and perhaps be more likely to finish) than some of the more traditional college texts. The LSC-North Harris library developed a pleasure reading collection with this same function. With the joint library, there would be no need for the expense and cataloging of a separate collection. Similarly at the MLK library, "education students have access to extensive children's and young adult collections for courses" (Marie 2007, 26).

A college or university library may feel the need to purchase materials that students would use in the rest of their lives, such as self-help or motivational items. For LSC-CyFair, not having to purchase these items allowed the collection development librarian to focus on purchasing scarce resources on curriculum issues. Librarians at the Front Range library have also been able to focus on curriculum issues. "We have found that about one fifth of the materials the college librarian selects from *Choice* reviews have already been purchased by the public library for the Harmony library (Dornseif 2001, 111). This is an older statistic, taken from 2000, but there is little reason to believe that the underlying attributes have changed. At the MLK library, due to the diversity of the surrounding neighborhood, the public library subscribes to a wide variety of newspapers, magazines, and other materials in foreign languages which also assists students studying those languages (Marie 2007, 26).

Prior to the joint agreements, the Harris County Public Library often purchased materials for the community college student. Students would frequent the county's libraries because they were familiar with the libraries, they were already going to the library with other family members, or the high-demand items they needed were already checked out at the community college library. Having a joint library collection assists with the first two considerations since it is now a one-stop location. In terms of the collection, some items that the public library would have selected for local community college students would not have to be purchased since the college would now be obtaining them. On the other hand, this reduction does not address the third issue mentioned previously—that college students visit the public library because items are unavailable at their campus library. However, by being part of an integrated system that transfers items between branches, it may be easier for students to request items from other locations.

Students can request from locations throughout the academic and public library systems in several of the libraries we queried. However, in at least one joint library, there are two separate circulation systems so that students cannot borrow from the public side, and vice versa. The long-term goal of that library is to have one integrated system, but at present it is not. We will discuss more about system integration issues that joint libraries face in the technology chapter.

With the LSC system, interlibrary loans are directed through either the public library system or the college district, depending on the type of library card. The public library was initially concerned that faculty and students would place a higher demand on the services and insisted that the college district handle the requests from students, faculty, and staff. Initially, requesting an interlibrary loan (ILL) was a perplexing process for patrons at the LSC-Tomball Library. Two different paper forms were used. The college required the patron to submit the ILL request in person and sign a multipage carbon form, while the county librarians took the ILL request both in person and by phone on a single 3-by-5-inch sheet form. Luckily, the library's use of technology has advanced and ILLs can now be requested directly online by patrons. The college website also helps the customer out by providing links to both the college's and the county library's ILL forms. If a patron selects the wrong form, the ILL departments now take care of it behind the scenes by electronically forwarding the request to the other partner.

SUCCESS

In the first six months the MLK library reached the circulation projections for the first year. An even bigger sign of the success of the merger is that students check out more of the public collection than they do of the academic collection. Conversely, the public patrons check out more of the academic collection.

The perception that library users have of the success of the joint library will in part be decided by how many more resources they have after the merger. If all patrons feel that they now have easy access to more materials than they did before, whether it is for faculty to get feature films or popular fiction or public patrons having great access to medical or scholarly databases, they will feel more positive about the joint library. A successful merger is dependent on the ongoing coordination and creation of an expanded and more comprehensive collection, but also on the careful attention to making sure the physical and online materials are visible and easy to access by all constituencies.

EIGHT

TECHNOLOGY AND TECHNICAL SERVICES

I'd be happy if I could think that the role of the library was sustained and even enhanced in the age of the computer.

—Bill Gates

As technology has advanced, computers have become more central to the mission of the library. There are many technical services and technology issues that arise in a joint library. Use of computers is an issue in any library and is only compounded in the joint library. Some aspects of this issue include the number of computers, filtering of computers, access to computers, plus hardware concerns if the computers are owned by different entities. There are other technology-related issues not related to the physical aspect of computers such as the merging of two catalogs and off-site library authentication. Because each library has its own particular technology challenges, this chapter will not attempt to answer specific technical issues, but instead will outline some of the general issues that arise.

NOT ENOUGH COMPUTERS

The proper number of computers available for patron use is a large concern and a large expense, and one for which there is not an easy answer. A joint library may have more computers than either entity would have had individually, but there are more patrons as well. Conversely, the different partners may decide that rather than combining the number of computers that each would have had individually, this would be an area in which they would decide to economize by reducing the overall number. Each library will still have a set amount of money to spend on computers, so a technology plan written specifically for the joint library is needed.

In a joint public/academic library, the usage patterns are slightly different, with the bulk of student usage coming during the day and public usage in the evenings and weekends (Kauppila and Russell 2003). This, however, does not mean there are not times of very high usage. This pattern of usage is somewhat thrown off during the summer when families and teens not in school increase the number of patrons wanting computers to use. College patterns of usage may change due to fluctuations in the number of students. At the LSC system, summer enrollments are high because students who are enrolled full-time at a university frequently take less expensive classes at the community college while they are home during the summer.

Of course, it is difficult to know how the changes in computing will affect the role of the library as a source of free access to computers. However, even though the increasing use of laptop and tablet computers may change some physical configurations, public libraries will probably still be the source of computer access for people who cannot afford a computer of their own. There will still be students needing access to computers while they are on campus.

One solution to the problem of more users than computers is a software program to reserve computers and enforce time limits on PCs. Of course, the verification of users can be a problem in a joint library where the users may have two different types of library cards—student IDs and public library cards. The verification software will need to accommodate this duality as well as address the privacy concerns of patrons who do not wish to log in with a card that personally identifies them. Some alternative, such as dummy cards, must be developed.

Students working on course work may resent others using computers for leisure activities when computers are at a premium, but this concern is certainly not limited to public users, since college students are just as likely to use computers for leisure activities. A time limit on the computer would affect research users disproportionately since it is easier to break off and resume a session on Facebook than stop in the middle of a complicated research session or composition of a term paper due that day. The time allotted to students may need to be longer. If the computers are funded and operated by separate entities, the computers may be segregated, with access limited to particular users. The disadvantage of this solution is that the seamless goal is compromised.

FILTERING

Filtering is one of the biggest concerns in joint libraries. Public libraries may be required to filter by the Children's Internet Protection Act, a state law, or a local requirement by the governing body. If they do not filter, the public still may have concerns about children accessing materials or viewing materials on PCs in the general area. For college students, there is a need for access to materials which might not be accessible on filtered computers. The solution at the joint library for Broward County and Nova Southeastern University is to have unfiltered computers but to have security officers who patrol the area for abuses. The Metropolitan Community College library at South Omaha has filtered computers because the computers are all purchased by the public library system. For years the Lone Star College system had a policy that children could not use computers without an adult present, which obviously needed to be changed when two of the campus libraries became joint facilities. The libraries each have areas of computers with filters and intended for children and teens. These computers are paid for and maintained by the public partner. Additionally there are many computers purchased by the college and maintained by its technology staff which are covered under the college district policy regarding computer use on campus. This policy includes the stipulation that students may not view "obscene materials" with the definition of obscene materials taken from the Texas statutes.

The issue of filtering came up at the Dr. Martin Luther King, Jr. Library in San Jose when one of the city councilors for San Jose was advocating the use of filters for the library. "However, the library is a joint-use facility with San Jose State University, whose administration is opposed to web filtering of any type." The *San Jose Mercury News* reported May 15, 2008, that San Jose State University President Don Kassing said in a letter to the city that installing filters would "violate the spirit of our joint operating agreement by restricting intellectual freedom." The operating agreement does not refer directly to filtering, but contains an endorsement of intellectual freedom and access to library materials. Of course, one of the arguments about Internet access and the library is whether the access should include everything available on the Internet. The agreement does spell out that if the public library did later choose to limit access to materials, such a limit would not apply to college materials, although this does not specify materials accessed via the Internet.

This is one example where the different missions of the different types of library may clash. Even though the agreement had spelled out a commitment to intellectual freedom, the different missions came to a head. According to an online article posted by *American Libraries,* the issue was resolved on the basis of budget, however, as the council voted not to spend the money on filtering software.

> SJSU Media Relations Director Pat Lopes Harris told *AL* that faculty "believe there should be no screening, either at King or the branches, unless we're consulted first as part of the operating agreement." Among the stumbling blocks she foresaw was the proposed login-screen message, which "is written in a somewhat threatening manner." Harris conceded, however, that the library and Academic Senate could probably come to an agreement on filtering children's workstations at the King Library since SJSU students do not use them. (May 9, 2009)

MAINTENANCE OF COMPUTERS

Joint libraries typically have the choice of each partner purchasing and maintaining its own computers or providing an allowance from one partner to the other for the computers. The MLK, LSC-Tomball, and LSC-CyFair libraries all have some computers owned by each entity and maintained by the separate information technology (IT) departments. There are some advantages to this method. First, the budget cycles are on different plans so there may be new computers from either budget at different times. Second, the computers may be on different servers so that when some are not working or being maintained there are still computers available for use. Third, there are some variations in the software available on the various PCs that gives patrons another option for use.

A disadvantage of the dual IT departments is the need to keep the two departments informed of what is happening with the other. At the LSC joint libraries, the public library's entire IT department is located off-site. The decision was made that all IT network-related problems and concerns with computers purchased by the county had to be referred to the county IT department. For librarians, this means an extra step in troubleshooting computers.

Authentication of library computers can sometimes be a concern. Access to library databases is usually verified by the IP address of the computer. In a large system such as Lone Star College, the IP addresses are not assigned to specific computers but are randomly assigned to computers as they are in use.

However, if the range of static IP addresses changes on the college computers, the public library's IT staff needs to be notified so that the computers will be verified as proper users. Otherwise, the patron, logging onto the computer in the library, will be improperly denied access to the databases. This is a matter of proper communication between the IT departments.

CATALOGING

Merging online catalogs can be a large technological hurdle. In terms of technical services, the biggest hurdle to merging the separate Horizon library systems for Harris County and Lone Star College was harmonizing the policy differences between the entities. Initially, at the LSC-CyFair library, the customers had to use two sets of library catalogs and the staff had to use two sets of circulation computers, one connected to the HCPL system and one connected to the LSC system. After the joint library was opened at LSC-Tomball, there was an additional incentive to push forward with the previous goal of a complete integration of the systems.

Since LSC (then North Harris Montgomery Community College District) already had a shared catalog and joint borrowing agreement with the Montgomery County Memorial Library System (MCMLS), the arrangements with the Harris County Public Library for the joint libraries of CyFair and Tomball had to be compatible with all three systems. The plan was for borrowers from the LSC-Tomball and LSC-CyFair libraries to have all the borrowing rights of HCPL and LSC, plus retain the ability to request items from the Montgomery County Memorial Library. However, neither HCPL nor MCMLS wanted their materials to be requested by all patrons in both counties. MCMLS was concerned about being dwarfed by the larger borrower base of Harris County, and HCPL was concerned about its unique items.

The technical services librarians and circulation managers met regularly to draw up spreadsheets of the intended usage by various borrower types, item types, and location. The libraries had different loan periods for different item types, such as a one-week checkout for DVDs and two-week checkouts for books. To further complicate things, LSC allowed faculty to check out books for the entire semester and Montgomery County allowed three-week checkouts for books. There was also the matter of resolving differences in how fines accrued. LSC faculty did not accrue fines, but students did, as did all other patron types. These are just a few examples of how the rules varied. Massive spreadsheets were compiled that outlined which rules applied in which situation. The circulation periods were standardized across the three library systems and there was an agreed-upon order of which rules took precedence: by location of checkout first, then borrower type, and then item type. Once the rules were determined on paper, then it was necessary to work with the Horizon catalog to make those various restrictions work. All the library districts already used the Horizon system, which simplified the process somewhat.

The MLK library had an even bigger technology problem to overcome since they used two different vendors for their library management systems. Initially each library wished to retain its own vendor, but a list of criteria from both libraries was developed into a Request for Proposal (RFP) and was sent to both the current vendors. Even though the vendor selected was one that was currently used by one library, there were new models and procedures, so in any event there were many adjustments and training that had to be done. Having a unified system paid off since the new MLK library has higher circulation than either previous library, making it one of the public libraries with the highest circulation in the country.

Although the majority of the meetings for the LSC merger were between the technical services librarians from the three systems, they were able to have some meetings with the library system directors who had the authority to set the guidelines. Luke Rosenberger, the automated library system librarian for the college district, credited the ability to have those key decision makers present to allow the proceedings to move forward in a timely manner because otherwise valuable time would have been lost shuttling back and forth with suggestions and counter-suggestions.

One potentially derailing roadblock was how fines or fees accrued by borrowers on items would be settled. If an LCS patron had material transferred from the MCMLS to LSC and then lost the item, the fines could be paid at the LSC library, even though the item was purchased by MCMLS. However, there was no mechanism in place to transfer money from LSC to MCMLS. Eventually it was decided to assume that such exchanges would even out. The Dr. Martin Luther King, Jr. Library in San Jose took the opposite approach in terms of fines. Fines for lost books are attributed to the owning institution and even "student financial obligations reported to the University registrar should not include transactions related to their use of public library materials" (R. Woods 2004, 207).

E-MAIL

It may seem commonplace that all the members should be able to communicate easily by e-mail, but at both the MLK and LSC joint libraries there are separate distribution lists. At the MLK library, the university and the city employ different e-mail systems (Lotus Notes and Microsoft Outlook) which are not seamlessly integrated. Initially LSC employees were not on distribution lists for the public library, and any new hire had to be notified to the public library. In an effort to unify the two staffs at LSC-Tomball, all of the Harris County Public Library employees were given college e-mail accounts and put on the campuswide distribution lists. Having to check their county e-mail accounts and college e-mail accounts daily became time-consuming for many employees and caused some grumbling over the amount of e-mail they received from the college that did not concern them. Most joint libraries find that there is a trial-and-error period in finding an efficient and effective way to communicate with all of the employees and key players that support the library, such as the IT department.

WEBSITE

The consideration for any joint library website is to reflect the dual nature of the library and yet make it easy for both sets of patrons to find the information they need. Obviously certain basic features such as hours, location, and so on are the same for either users, but databases and events are targeted to different users. In an ideal situation one website would showcase everything but allow different users to get what they need in just a click or two. The Alvin Sherman Library at Nova Southeastern University (NSU) lists headings for NSU community and the Broward County Community as well as a sidebar of activities that include events for a wide variety of users. However, because many joint libraries are part of a system or district, they may need to conform to the websites for those entities.

The LSC joint libraries are on both the LSC libraries website and the HCPL website, although in the case of the public library site there is little recognition of the joint use features. The joint libraries are listed just like any other branch. Initially the LSC-CyFair library website was for that library only and was able to highlight the library's dual nature. As the college district consolidated the five campus library websites into one Lone Star College library website, there were concerns from the other campuses, which were strictly community college libraries, about listing children and teen programs. A compromise was reached, and the current website lists library services for children, teens, adults, students, and faculty. All databases available at the joint libraries are listed (in categories and alphabetically) with designations for who can access them off-site.

One possible solution is to have two different database sites for the two different categories of users. Typically, library databases are accessible to everyone in the joint library, but off-site access is limited to cardholders from the particular institution that funds the database. However, since the website is the primary portal for users in the library to access databases, if each site listed only college databases or only public databases, patrons might not be aware of all the resources they have available to them, thus negating one of the advantages of the joint library. However, it is also necessary for the person who maintains the website to be continually informed about changes in databases by both purchasing institutions.

CUSTOMIZED LOG-INS

Of course, technology changes are more rapid than in other areas of the library. Doug Caesar, manager of user services at LSC-CyFair , offered the opinion that even in the relatively short eight years that the LSC-CyFair library has been open, technological advances have changed the ways users access online resources. One advance is the development of individual log-ins and customized portals for the various users. Each person upon logging into the computer would have a setup for their user type. This is part of the trend of cloud computing which allows the PC to behave more as a terminal and less as a processor. This development may also extend the life of the PCs (Caesar, pers.comm.). However, it would still be necessary for patrons of joint libraries to have a portal that reflects the wider variety of resources available to them as opposed to users at locations which are members of only one agency.

Since there are many technical concerns that arise in the development of a joint library, depending on the size of the project and the budgets involved, it may advisable or necessary to hire a consultant or manager for the merger. Richard Woods (2004, 209) of the MLK library states that if he had to do the merger over again, he "would have insisted on an on-site, full-time project manager to implement the new shared library system," rather than a consultant to assist. The technical personnel who must implement or manage the new system may not be employees of the joint library but work for a parent entity. Thus it is critical that the upper management of the parent entity support the merger of the libraries to ensure proper buy-in from the technical staff since they may not share the vision. However, if the vision is well communicated to all employees, even nonlibrary staff will take pride in the joint project and participate in the endeavor.

NINE

CASE STUDIES

*We never know how high we are / Til we
are called to rise / And then, if we are true
to plan, / Our statures touch the skies.*

—Emily Dickinson

We chose several different projects to study somewhat in depth to learn about best practices and pitfalls.

The Dr. Martin Luther King, Jr. Library, a project between San Jose State University and the city of San Jose, is often seen as a model of success where two distinctly different entities thrive side by side.

Lone Star College-CyFair Branch Library of the Harris County Public Library and the Lone Star College-Tomball Community Library are home base for our authors. We decided to describe our experiences in depth because two different management models were selected for these joint libraries.

The University Branch–Sugar Land of the Fort Bend County Library System has a model which seems to be in vogue lately. Instead of trying to coexist with another entity, it is one large public library which, for a price, happens to serve the University of Houston and the Wharton County Junior College.

The North Lake Community Library, a joint project of the city of Irving and North Lake College in Texas, is a classic case of a "glorious failure" (Lamar Veatch, pers. comm.). We spoke to some key players in that endeavor and attempt to understand the factors that led to this famous breakup.

Finally, we look at the upcoming joint library between the city of Virginia Beach and the Tidewater Community College. We use this case study to develop our own criteria for success and to predict whether this project will succeed.

CASE STUDY
Dr. Martin Luther King, Jr. Library

A Joint Project between San Jose State University
and the City of San Jose, California

"A watershed event in collaborative libraries occurred in June 2004 with the awarding of the prestigious Gale/Library Journal 2004 Library of the Year Award to the Dr. Martin Luther King, Jr. Library in San Jose, California. This complex, highly visible, and initially highly suspect project demonstrates that two existing libraries with their different missions, different clients, and different bureaucracies can share not only a building, but also successfully integrate operations" (Breivik, Budd, and Woods 2005, 401).

BRINGING TOWN AND GOWN TOGETHER

San Jose State University lies in the middle of the city of San Jose. Perceived ivory tower aloofness and lack of community spirit led two leaders to forge a new innovative partnership. In February 1996 the mayor of San Jose, Susan Hammer, and the university president, Robert L. Caret, announced the joint library project (Guernsey 1998, A25). Their vision was to make the university more a part of the metropolitan area and share resources with overlapping constituencies. It was an exciting time with all the planning and choices to be made. Because of the complexity of the differences in the two entities, they decided to have employees from both parties in the same building rather than have one entity do all of the hiring. Seamless service was a priority; none of the users of the library would know if they were being served by the city's or university's employees. They decided not to commingle the circulating collections. Reference collections would merge as would reference service (Guernsey 1998). Differing vacation days, benefits, and pay scales would remain in place. If it was a city vacation day, the college employees would work and vice versa. Patricia Breivik, the former dean of the University Library, in her article "We're Married! The Rewards and Challenges of Joint Libraries," writes: "Creating a new organizational structure that has city and university employees working together in integrated units has been complex, and helping employees thrive in their new environment is an ongoing challenge" (Breivik, Budd, and Woods 2005, 402). The article goes into detail about the people issues that pop up and how there can be resentment when one side is perceived as more equitable. As time passes, new employees are hired who are aware of the pros and cons of each entity, and these resentments lessen. The director of the public side and the dean of the university side work together to enhance the mission of both institutions.

UNCERTAINTY BREWS FEAR

Some university personnel voiced fears that this would be just another large public library and the university would lose its primary academic resource. "Administrators speak of innovative partnerships and customer service, while professors wonder whether traditional resources for teaching and research are somehow being shortchanged in the quest to keep up with corporate trends" (Guernsey 1998, A25). There was an organized protest by the faculty as construction plans were under way. They formed a group called "Save Our University Library!" and ordered 250 blue buttons with SOUL! in yellow letters and held a protest rally that drew several hundred people. Scary stories of rug rats and sticky fingers circulated, and there were fears that students couldn't get access to computers and the public would check out all the university research materials. Five hundred signatures were collected to persuade the faculty senate to recommend a halt to the project. The president decided to go ahead despite the opposition. Administrators saw little evidence that the public would want the books needed by students and professors. A memorandum of understanding was circulated that stated "faculty members and students will have the right to recall books checked out by other library users; professors will have extended checkout privileges; and if the university deems that professors are having trouble getting access to its books, the city will be obligated to help alleviate the problem" (Guernsey 1998, A25). San

Jose's university librarian, C. James Schmidt, knew that this project was high profile enough to entice funding from the trustees when previously funding had just not been available. On the other side of the picture, "librarians also worry about a clash of cultures at the reference desk: An academic librarian makes a concerted effort not to do all of the work for the students, who are supposed to be learning how to conduct research. But the goal of a public reference librarian is to serve patrons, even if that means finding answers to obscure, research-intensive questions. Will staff members at the reference desk be expected to do both?" (Guernsey 1998, A25).

Construction began, the library was finished, and at first the university librarians were not required to staff the reference desk. They would take referrals if they were needed. This seems to show that the two cultures were not merged in the beginning and reveals a crack in the goal to remain seamless. According to Ruth Kifer, dean of libraries at San Jose State University, at present, however, because of layoffs due to funding issues, all librarians work the desk (Ruth Kifer, pers. comm.). This seems like a more equitable arrangement.

After many years of successful operation, it's now hard to find anyone who will admit to being opposed to this partnership, states current public library director Judith Light in a 2008 online video (Light 2008). She further states that one thing that helped with collection worries is Link Plus, a consortium of academic and public libraries in California and Nevada which shares materials. Even if materials were checked out at the Martin Luther King, Jr. Library, a book could get delivered in two days through the Link Plus service.

This library is often used as a model for other joint projects. It has been successful and award winning. Having two entities working side by side can be challenging, but in this case it has worked well. Tidewater Community College and the City of Virginia Beach are planning their new joint library, and they are modeling it after San Jose. While they probably will still have two payrolls, they decided not to keep the collections separate and will have all the library staff report to one academic library director.

CASE STUDY
Lone Star College-CyFair Branch

A Joint Project of the Harris County Public Library
and the Lone Star College System

It was a hot, humid September afternoon in west Houston when college President Diane Troyer approached County Commissioner Steve Radack about extending West Road so the new Cy-Fair College would have vehicle access on the south. As conversation ensued, Radack mentioned that he had funds to build a 30,000-square-foot public library around the Katy Prairie near where the brand-new Cy-Fair College would sit. A seed of an idea was planted in their minds.

The architectural plans for the 50,000-square-foot college library had already been drawn up. Most administrators would have dismissed the idea of a public library in a college as out of hand and a little too late. However, this radical concept fit right in with Troyer's vision—a college which would teach students to embrace change, to be innovative, to collaborate, to take part in their community, to take chances. The space where the future library stood would have to be reworked to accommodate a public library. For example, the architectural plans had the entrance to the library in the center of campus,

LSC-CyFair Library exterior. Photo by Amy Willis.

around the large water fountain feature. A public library would require easy access from the street for children and mothers with baby carriages. Not only would there be more work and expense to rework the architectural plans, but there would also be the need to create an entirely new concept for the library on campus.

This idea was controversial and risky. Comments received stated that the mission of a public library versus an academic library were too different to allow a successful combination library. How would service to children fit in with an academic library? Would students be served as well as those in a strictly college library? How would faculty react? This concept attacked the fundamental assumption that college and public libraries are two entirely different entities. Public libraries are supported by taxpayers, college libraries are supported by student tuition and fees. Public libraries are noisy, college libraries are quiet, elegant ivory towers. Public libraries are for fun reading, college libraries are for serious research.

Troyer and her leadership team decided to embrace change and challenge those assumptions. Why let tired, hackneyed assumptions limit the CyFair vision? Why not build a bigger and better library with a new mission, one that looked forward to the new millennium, not back at nineteenth-century concepts of the library?

LSC-CyFair Library adult computer area. Photo by Amy Willis.

Collaboration and sharing are always a challenge. It's easier to do it yourself, the way you have always done it. When Lone Star College-CyFair (then Cy-Fair College as part of the North Harris Montgomery Community College District) was created by a bond issue, it was to be the fifth college in the system, slated to open on August 25, 2003. This would be the first new comprehensive college being built in the United States in the twenty-first century. A team of visionaries and educators crafted a mission that included collaboration, innovation, and change. The following statement would be a mantra for staff as they forged ahead: Lone Star College-CyFair is a responsive, innovative, and collaborative learning community that thrives on preparing students for a lifetime of learning and change.

The library was to be part of a learning commons, along with tutoring. Counselors were right around the corner helping with school and career planning. An assistive technology lab also was part of the commons. A steering committee was formed consisting of Vice President Earl Campa, Deputy Director Rhoda Goldberg, and others reporting to President Troyer and the public library director, Catherine Park. The library steering committee knew that this library would have to support faculty and students and now the local community as well. Instead of handing over the running of the library to the county, the team crafted an agreement. Because of accreditation issues,

LSC-CyFair Library cybercafe. Photo by Earl Campa.

the steering committee did not want to relinquish the library to the public library. It felt that in order to have a college-level library, academic librarians were needed. The county wanted to be sure that the library director had public library experience. The agreement drawn up for this joint project spelled out the details (see appendix A for the full agreement). Harris County Library Director Catherine Park knew that this was her chance to build a new library in the northwest area on the Katy Prairie. Thus, she and Troyer shared a common vision for their new library—not just a public library and not just a college library. Pragmatism on both sides to make it work prevailed (Diane K. Troyer, pers. comm.).

The architectural plans had to be reworked and the county agreed to pay the college $1 million for these costs: redesign and reengineering of the college library, the ordering of additional structural steel, the expansion of the foundation work, and the paving of 150 additional parking spaces (North Harris Montgomery Community College District Financial Report and Consideration No. 20. 2002). The Gilbane Construction Company was also paid $3,590 in additional funds for the redesign (North Harris Montgomery Community College District Financial Report and Consideration No. 6. 2002). In the revised plans, the new square footage would be 78,500 and the entrance to the library would be moved from the center of campus to the parking lot on the south side of campus.

LSC-CyFair Library children's room. Photo by Earl Campa.

A summary of the agreement:

> "This Joint Library will provide a unique service to area residents and college students in that the shared operation will provide more, enhanced opportunities than either entity could offer separately" (Williams 2002).

> "Governance of this shared operation will be through a Joint Steering Committee reporting to the Cy-Fair College President and the Director of the Harris County Public Library System" (Williams 2002).

> Harris County will provide construction funds required for redesign and appropriate furniture and equipment.

> All staff will be employees of the district; the county will pay the college the cost normally paid by a county branch library.

> Collections will be uniquely provided by both sides to meet each constituent's needs. The collection will be cataloged using the Dewey Decimal System. The county will provide cataloguing and circulation functions.

> Harris County contributed $1.3 million for the start-up collection. The college contributed $290,000 for curriculum-related purchases (Achen 2003, 1).

The steering committee addressed a variety of issues.

QUALITY OF TEACHING

One adjunct faculty member asked her mentor, a founding faculty member and first faculty senate president, Heather Mitchell, "Since it's a public library, do we get quality research instruction for our students?" Mitchell quickly assured her that this team of librarians was experienced and dedicated to providing quality instruction. While not every librarian had teaching experience, every one of them made it a priority to engage students and teach them to think critically about resources and to promote academic integrity. If this were strictly a public library, the faculty senate president might not have been resolute in her assurance to the faculty member.

FILTERING

College libraries pride themselves on providing information with no restriction. It's part of academic freedom not to limit a student's access to information. Public libraries filter computers so that patrons cannot access pornography and sometimes social media sites. At CyFair, the children's room computers and the teen computers are filtered. The college president, Diane Troyer, did not want the other public computers filtered, nor did her boss, the college district's chancellor, John Pickelman. The librarians at CyFair accepted this decision, but were quick to respond if there were complaints about disturbing content on the computers. The computers all had the following terms of use notice posted on the desktop.

> The display or transmission of messages, images, or cartoons that are sexually explicit or that demean a person on the basis of race, ethnicity, gender, national origin, religion, or sexual orientation may constitute prohibited harassment and are prohibited under LSCS Board Policies AHB and DAB.
>
> Violation of these policies may result in the loss of computer use privileges, dismissal or other appropriate legal actions.

One concern was that children of all ages use the computers, but the library did not have the staff to constantly monitor children's use. This concern turned out to be unfounded since there was little abuse of the content. The college district's library policy states that no unaccompanied children under eighteen may use the computers. A decision was made not to restrict those under eighteen's access to computers, effectively adopting the public library policy that permits children to use the computers.

CENSORSHIP

So many academic libraries fear the ugly head of censorship. Librarians in general prefer to allow all sorts of books and materials for their constituents. Occasionally a book selection will be questioned. For example, some teen books by Judy Blume dealing with coming-of-age issues have parents demanding their removal from the library. Teen Librarian Elise Sheppard says that usually in cases like this, the library would change the book from a teen book to an adult book if the complaint is deemed valid (Elise Sheppard, pers. comm.).

Intellectual freedom has never become an issue at CyFair. However, as the dean of libraries at the University of Houston says, some academic libraries cite the possibility of censorship threats as a reason not to have academic libraries running a joint library (Dana Rook, pers. comm.).

CREATIVE PROGRAMMING: A SERENDIPITOUS HAPPENING

The new CyFair Library had all sorts of librarians hired. There were academic librarians, public librarians, children's librarians, a teen librarian, a museum librarian, and school librarians. The book clubs were immediately established as far as adult programs went. There was a mystery book club, women of the world, and a sports page book club. The children's librarians were way ahead of the curve with sundry story times and craft times. No one, however, had been hired to be the programming librarian. The assistant director was in charge of this area, but at first it was considered enough to have the college library instruction classes designated as adult programs.

The college opened in August 2003, and it was abuzz with activity, ideas, celebrations, and dreams of what was to come. In late October, one of the counselors, Jadi Johnson, a real firecracker who cut her teeth on leading-edge programs at the Tomball campus, approached the teen librarian, Elise Sheppard, a librarian known for innovative teen programs and a knack for making things happen. "I have an idea that can realize the dream of our community to become part of this campus of lifelong learning." Sheppard was intrigued and Johnson continued. "Let's create an educational environment like none other. Something free, educational, entertaining, welcoming, rewarding, and empowering. Perhaps a weekly class for all adults in our community." Elise Sheppard then brought this idea to the reference librarians (Gunnels 2009, 4).

Jadi Johnson's idea was a catalyst for creative change. Her vision was for a welcoming atmosphere where the community could come without cost and explore educational opportunities and, perhaps, take college classes. Soon a very successful program was born: LIFE (Learning Inspiration Fellowship and Enrichment) as a weekly program on Wednesdays from 10 to 11 a.m. Ken Doherty, an avid LIFEr, describes its impact: "The regularity of the program, most every Wednesday morning something good is likely to be found at the library, encourages it to become a habit and much easier to remember. It has had a beneficial social function, allowing several of the regulars to get to know each other, an important benefit for the older people who can end up alone all too easily" (Gunnels 2009, 3).

More and more programs, such as gaming for adults, English as a Second Language Classes, Wii bowling, and business success seminars, are adding to the variety of the adult programs. Computer classes in English and Spanish are popular in the community as well. The teen librarian started a prom dress drive for needy teens and it has been sustained for years and is going strong. One librarian is the liaison to the local school district. She has book clubs and classes to train the school librarians.

FRIENDS OF THE LIBRARY

Since all the branches of the Harris County Public Library system had individual Friends groups, the CyFair branch was encouraged by the HCPL administration to have one as well. There was some research to determine if any community colleges had Friends of the Library groups. Eventually the model was based more on other HCPL groups and bylaws were drawn up. Possible members were recruited from different constituencies such as retired persons, homeschooling parents, and the college community. The major difference was that money raised was given to the North Harris Montgomery Community College District Foundation (now Lone Star College Foundation) with a separate spending code. This action permitted the Friends group to use the foundation's 501(c)(3) status, without having to apply on its own as a nonprofit organization, plus it made it easier to spend the money since it stayed within the college system.

The Friends group operates a separate room in the library where they collect and sell donated books. The Friends group funds traditional items such as the summer reading programs and teen books, but they also sponsor other causes such as a student library research scholarship award given to students who demonstrate the best use of resources for their research papers.

FINES

The college district's policy of not fining faculty and staff for overdue items at its other four campus libraries was carried over to the joint library at CyFair. Due to the joint library partnership, the fine money would be kept by the library and used for extra funding for programs and materials, which was a change in the fine policy for both the college and Harris County.

TERRITORIALITY

People still ask the staff, "Do you work for the college or the county?" They reply, "Both!" All are paid by the college, but Harris County has an equal interest in the success of this library. The HCPL administration dictates what children's programs must be in place and have certain requirements for the teen programs as well. They are more laissez-faire with the adult side, but they do ask that certain celebrations be acknowledged. For example, HCPL wants an actual program to be created for African-American History Month. The county has a rule that all librarians must have twenty hours of professional development each year. This rule does not apply to the joint library as they are employees of the college. However, these librarians usually have much more than twenty hours per year, making it a moot point. Since all of the librarians were hired with the joint library in mind, they were screened for the desire to make this a success.

A HICCUP

When hiring the first director, the county insisted on five years of public library experience (later changed to three years). The college wanted someone with community college experience. The salary level was low for a library of this size and complexity. Librarians with both types of experience and a history of successful supervision were not applying. Consequently, the library director was not hired until approximately one month before the library opened, after several other librarian positions were filled. Since her background had been in public libraries, she pushed the library in that direction and received lukewarm support from the other campus library directors. She also experienced internal dissension because the librarians felt they were ordered around like members of the typing pool instead of honoring the college's tradition of having faculty (which the librarians were) participate in the decision making. Unsuccessful in blending the talents of the librarians and creating an atmosphere that reflected one library, she left. The assistant director, Mick Stafford, assumed the director's position and had enough college and public library experience to make his vision a truly blended library. It is thus important to have a committed director on board early who will not encourage territoriality or favor one side of the partnership.

WEB PAGE

The Harris County Public Library has a standard web template for each of the branches. It lists the equipment in each branch, the branch's hours, its programs, and the name of the branch manager. There are slide shows of pictures of the branch. When the LSC-CyFair Branch Library was formed, one CyFair librarian, Monica Norem, originally from the college's North Harris campus, had the idea to create another web page which had the look of the college. It would give the library more flexibility to provide information needs to faculty, students, and staff as well as the community. She lobbied the web administrator of the college to give her access to the Web. With input from other librarians, she designed a website that included names and contact information of all library employees, a list of all the computer software on the more than 200 computers in the library, a form for faculty to request instruction, and much more. Another reason for the new web page was that the college subscribed to databases not shown on the county's web page. This forward-thinking librarian contributed immensely to information availability and ease of use of this library.

CHANGE OF LEADERSHIP

The library has been operating since August 2003. Its entire leadership team of three vice presidents and president has changed. One of our criteria of success is to have strong support both at the leadership level and grassroots level. We interviewed the current president, Audre Levy, to see how she views this joint library. Her office overlooks the 78,500-square-foot library with over 200 computers. She is amazed at all the activity and usage. However, from her point of view, it looks like one large computer lab. Levy also has concerns that students may not find access to a computer when most of the computers are used for gaming (Audre Levy, pers. comm.).

We also had an interesting glitch involving one of the new vice presidents. The teen librarian applied for a sabbatical involving a project to get teens college-ready. The vice president read the proposal and felt it was not appropriate for a college sabbatical since it dealt with pre-college students. The proposal was not sent on to the sabbatical committee as a result. This attitude shows a lack of understanding of the joint library, which is a partnership in all ways. The teen librarian is every bit as much of a professor as the adult librarians and children's librarians. This type of misunderstanding can undermine the partnership. Some joint libraries are not willing to confront this type of issue and choose to have either entity run the library entirely on its own. This does simplify management, but fails to tap the riches of a true partnership of both types of libraries.

BUDGET TROUBLE

Texas is facing a budget crisis and it devolves to the local government. The college is funded less and less by the state, and this is forcing the college to cut its budget. They have already implemented a hiring "chill." Harris County has seen dramatically reduced revenues due to falling property rates. HCPL has laid off eight full-time employees in the system. The college has announced that it intends to protect all full-time jobs as it deals with the budget reductions. Since the library is funded by both parties, it is unclear how this will play out. If Harris County withholds funds because of a budget crisis, it may be in breach of contract and the partnership could be in jeopardy. It is hoped that this would not occur. It is still unknown if this branch is protected because of this unique arrangement. In 2007 the Alvin Sherman Library almost had a divorce when Broward County sought to lower its yearly contribution by 9 percent as all other county libraries were required. (See the concluding chapter for more details on this budgetary crisis.)

A SUCCESS STORY

This library has been a success beyond anyone's expectations. The college now serves almost 20,000 students and the Lone Star College system serves almost 80,000 in all. This library has been an important part of the community. Over 6 million items have been checked out since it opened in August 2003. It invites children and teens onto campus and they often turn into students of the college. In the initial Southern Association of Colleges and Schools (SACS) accreditation report for the college, it was commended for the community library. In these troubled budgetary times, the library has postponed hiring one retired librarian and there are cuts in operating costs that are being made. However, a robust Friends of the Library, dedicated librarians and staff, and a happy community of voters gives hope that the library will survive the storm.

CASE STUDY
Lone Star College-Tomball Community Library
A Joint Project with the Harris County Public Library
and the Lone Star College System

In 2000 the North Harris Montgomery Community College District (NHMCCD) passed a capital bond referendum and began working with architects on designing new buildings for its Tomball Campus, including an expansion of its library and extended learning center which included the college's tutoring and testing services and volunteer center. (NHMCCD was renamed in 2007 and is today known as Lone Star College.) In June 2001, and less than three miles away, the Harris County Public Library demolished its 6,000-square-foot Tomball Branch and temporarily moved the library operations to a vacant store in a nearby shopping center. HCPL's plan was to construct a new facility on the old library site with additional adjoining land donated by the City of Tomball. Harris County held a groundbreaking ceremony in November 2001 for the expanded 15,000-square-foot public library branch. A month later, the excitement over the new public library was washed away when engineers discovered a high water table on the site. At first there were hopes that the site could be remediated, but the estimates for re-engineering the project for the wet soil conditions quickly soared to over $500,000. The community was disheartened when the county announced its decision to halt construction of the library in March 2002.

During this same time period, the North Harris Montgomery Community College District was receiving overwhelmingly positive accolades in response to its plan to build a joint library with the Harris County Public Library at the new CyFair campus it was constructing in Cypress, Texas, a rapidly growing area of Harris County. In May 2002, as options for building a new public library branch in Tomball seemed to be disappearing, a member of the Tomball City Council, Diane Holland, suggested building a joint library to Ray Hawkins, the president of NHMCCD's Tomball College Campus, and the Harris County commissioner for the Tomball area, Jerry Eversole. Both Hawkins and Eversole immediately supported the idea of constructing a joint facility on the campus of Tomball College. Within months both had secured additional funds (for a total of $13.1 million), which enabled the architectural firm Page Southerland Page to redesign the plans for a much larger and more modern library than either entity had initially planned.

GRASSROOTS PROTEST

What appeared to be a win-win situation for all parties, however, triggered a determined grassroots effort to stop the joint library and keep the county library branch in what was considered the more convenient downtown area of Tomball. Despite the critical outcry, both the county commissioner and the college president were steadfast in moving the project forward. Both sent a clear and loud message to the community that the new library would welcome and meet the needs of all of its users. Gilbane Construction Company broke ground for the facility in September 2003 and fifteen months later gave the college the go-ahead to start moving in.

Due to the concerted public relations efforts of the college and the county, the community dissension which had overshadowed the start of the project evaporated by the time of the library's grand opening in January 2005. Both public and college library users were ecstatic over their new 72,000-square-foot, two-story, glass-front facility with large fountains at the front and rear entrances; a vibrantly colored children's reading and program area; a meeting room large enough to hold groups of 125; heavily staffed customer service desks for reference and circulation on both floors; a relaxing young adult room furnished with beanbag chairs, DVD players, and headphones; a long corridor of group study rooms filled with natural lighting; three computer-equipped classrooms tucked away in the back corners of the building; over 150 Internet-equipped computer stations; a well-stocked coffee bar; the college's tutoring and testing centers; plus a full-service drive-up window for those wanting to avoid the oppressive Texas summer heat.

A DIFFERENT APPROACH

Although both of the joint libraries at Tomball and CyFair were funded by the same college system and the same county library system, the decision was made early in the negotiations to find a different operating model for Tomball and to not try to replicate the CyFair fully integrated library model (which had not opened yet). The development of the Tomball joint library involved numerous brainstorming sessions, visits to other joint public/college librar-ies in California, Florida, Colorado, and Texas, input from community focus groups, and sometimes tense meetings between the two library partners. It was much easier for the CyFair Library to be fully integrated because it was built as part of a brand-new campus. The CyFair joint library proposal had been embraced more quickly because there were not any traditions that would be lost, operating routines to revamp, materials to re-catalog, or employees who would be negatively affected by being moved to a different retirement system, pay scale, or job title. In contrast, the Tomball College Library had been in existence since 1988, and the public library had operated in various locations in Tomball since 1961. The internal apprehension the two libraries faced was predictable because both the college library and the county branch library in Tomball had fervent supporters, long-term employees, tremendous pride in the personalized customer service each provided, and collections that each had strived for many years to acquire. Despite their close proximity, the two libraries also lacked a history of past collaborative experiences to build on. The strong internal and external resistance to the idea of a merged library forced the partners to carefully examine and evaluate which operating structure would best fit the Tomball joint library and nurture its success.

Instead of adopting the CyFair organizational structure with all of the employees hired by the college and managed by a single director who reported to both institutions, the Tomball agreement designated two codirectors, each reporting to her own parent institution. Both parties would contribute to the construction and furnishing of the building. The college would own and maintain the building, and the county would pay an annual operating fee to the college. Each partner was to hire, supervise, and evaluate its own employees, purchase and maintain its own collection, retain its current classification system for materials (Dewey Decimal for the public library and Library of Congress for the college), and operate its own computer network and public access stations. Unresolved conflicts between the two codirectors were to be brought to a governing committee made up of higher-level administrators from both entities. If the higher-level administrators could not come to an agreement, final resolution would be decided by the college's president and the county commissioner.

CODIRECTOR VS. CODIRECTOR

Along with the stated differences outlined in the contractual agreements, there were other striking differences in the operating methods and procedures that had to be reconciled—some quickly and some incrementally—to avoid patron friction and perpetual staff upheaval.

The two codirectors, Mary Jean Webster for the college and Wendy Schneider for the county, were both appointed in late 2004, just a few months before the grand opening in 2005. The two codirectors came with years of experience with their respective institutions and open eyes to the challenges ahead. Expecting to be in constant consultation with each other, they were placed in adjoining offices in the new building. Webster and Schneider spent the first couple of years working out many compromises to overcome the conflicts in the day-to-day operations, and they remained true to their promise to create a library that offered seamless customer services to all of its users. The changes that they gradually implemented led to more interaction and consolidation of efforts between the two staffs. One of their best tactics was to rely on customer feedback (both positive and negative) and actual usage patterns as the impetus for many of the changes. Keeping the changes tied to the needs of the customers made the shifts in policies and procedures easier for the two staffs to accept since they took the focus off of which side had the upper hand. By the third year the library was open, the two codirectors and the two staffs understood each other's values, operating rhythms, institutional priorities, and flash points. By then the two codirectors needed less guidance from the governing committee on how to handle the routine events that occurred in the joint library and never had an issue escalate to the higher levels of the review process. The two codirectors made it a point to share information on long-term plans or new initiatives that each was expected to incorporate into the library and to share the information with their respective staffs through e-mail and combined staff meetings.

START-UP CIRCULATION ISSUES

Initially it was seen as a significant problem that the county library placed its bar codes on the front outside book covers to make self-checkouts easier while the college's bar codes were placed on the inside back covers. Since both sides wanted to maintain uniformity with the other libraries in its own system, and neither side had the time, staff, or money to re-bar code its entire collection, the remedy was to leave the bar codes where they were and wait and see what the real impact was. As it turned out, the impact on the library's users was minimal due to the heavy staff presence near the self-checkout stations. The immediate staff help revealed the hidden bar codes and enabled users to quickly complete their checkouts. The silver lining in the bar code quandary was that it motivated both the college and HCPL to investigate RFID tag systems and serve as pilot RFID locations for their larger institutions.

The checkout routine was further complicated by the fact that the college and the public library also used different security tag systems to control the loss of materials. This again was expected to cause difficulties for patrons because the public library relied heavily on self-checkout machines while the college's circulation personnel manually desensitized the items to be checked out. The compromise that the codirectors worked out so patrons could check out all of their materials at a single checkout location was that new security strips were placed in all of the materials in the college's collection, a significantly smaller collection than the county library's and thus a smaller cost.

Another hurdle to smooth circulation operations was how audiovisual (AV) materials were handled and circulated. Only the faculty had checkout privileges for a large portion of the college's AV collection, plus the college used plastic lock boxes on all its audiovisual materials to limit the loss of expensive curriculum-related materials. The Harris County Public Library relied heavily on self-checkout, and their popular AV titles were much more affordable to purchase and replace, so they did not feel the need to use the security boxes. The county only restricted minors from checking out their AV materials. A three-pronged solution evolved: (1) the audiovisual collections were housed on separate floors; (2) signage was placed throughout the college's AV collection identifying the materials that could be circulated and segregating them from the "faculty only" materials; and (3) additional opening devices for the locked boxes were eventually purchased for the first-floor circulation area to avoid having to send a patron back upstairs to have circulating items unlocked.

The handling of periodicals was one more area of conflicting circulation policies. The public library circulated back issues of its periodicals, while the college allowed only in-house use of its entire periodical collection. To limit patron confusion, the periodical collections were maintained on separate floors and duplicate subscriptions were canceled. The declining usage of the college's print periodicals led the college librarians to reexamine the necessity of a noncirculating periodical policy in a library with an abundance of materials with online and remote full-text access. After consultations with the Tomball College teaching faculty, the policy was changed in 2009 so that the majority of the college's print periodicals could be checked out.

In the Tomball joint library, some of the operating routines that had been in place for years and were carefully protected during the planning stages for the joint library were abandoned rather quickly after the joint library opened. The college reserve desk, for example, had always been the place where faculty and students picked up items they had requested from other library locations after personally being notified of their arrival by phone by the circulation staff. After several confusing episodes when both college and community patrons could not find the hold items they requested in the new library, the decision was made to discontinue a separate pickup location for college materials and consolidate the hold pickup area in one convenient, self-serve location near the front door on the first floor. Because of the large volume of items being held for patrons, phone calls for pickup items were limited to college faculty, many of whom later enthusiastically opted for e-mail notification. The relocation of the holds also helped balance the workload for the college's circulation staff that had only two full-time and two part-time employees while the public library had more than twenty circulation/shelving assistant positions.

REFERENCE JITTERS

With the exception of the children's programming and the college reserve desk, all reference and circulation staffs were cross-trained and expected to handle any inquiries from a college or public library patron. Initially there were some territorial issues over who should handle a "college" or "public" library question. Feelings of uneasiness diminished primarily due to the informal sharing of expertise among the public and college librarians who worked side by side at the single reference desk located on the second floor. There were also attitude adjustments on how reference questions should be answered. The county reference librarians were trained to look up the item requested, find the call number for the item, and place the hold requests for the users. The college librarians typically used the reference questions as a teachable moment to show the user how to search the catalog or online databases, locate the items they needed, and place their own hold requests. Despite the differences in reference techniques, most of the librarians admitted they were on a steep learning curve and eagerly collaborated with their new colleagues to find the best resources in either collection. After the first year or so, the librarians felt comfortable handling the wide array of questions and customer expectations.

COMPUTER ACCESS POLICIES

Computers access was the area where patrons took notice of the distinct differences in how the two units in the joint library operated. The public access computers owned by the county were all filtered, required patrons to log in with a guest or library card bar code, had two-hour time limits, and several other downloading/document-saving restrictions. The college-owned computers were located on the same floor and were unfiltered, required no long-ins, were on a faster network, had several units with attached scanners, and, most important, from a user standpoint, had no time limits. Committed to providing seamless service, the policy adopted by the joint library codirectors was that any patron could use any computer, so there were no signs identifying one set of computers from the other. In no time at all, patrons of all ages migrated to the less restrictive college computers. The usage of college-owned computers ballooned even more when teens discovered that the public library computers blocked access to their favorite social networking sites. Other than relocating minors or parents with crying babies because of complaints about behavior or noise levels, the reference staff let users pick the computer stations that best fit their needs. Because there was an ample supply of computers and no one had to wait to use one, the public library eventually removed the time restriction on all of its computers at Tomball, except for those in the children's area, and turned off the never-used computer reservation station.

From the staff standpoint, having two computer networks turned out to be a real advantage. If one system crashed or was taken down for scheduled maintenance or upgrades, the reference staff could resettle users on the other's bank of computers in minutes or move their scheduled library instruction session to the other classroom. The disadvantage of two networks was that each had its own poorly visible print stations, with slightly different log-in requirements and systems of identifying documents. Printing on two networks required considerable staff intervention and considerable delays for patrons who went to the wrong print station to retrieve their documents. As part of the joint library agreement, the college's information technology staff was designated as the "first responders" for computer equipment and network issues for both the college and county library. On paper, it looked like a sensible and efficient way to keep both networks running since the county library's IT staff was housed near downtown Houston, thirty miles south of Tomball. In actuality, using the college IT personnel as the first level of contact typically just added another layer of people who logged the information and notified the county library's IT staff that there was a problem. Downtime periods for county-owned computers were not reduced because the college's IT staff lacked the authorizations needed to access the server, update software, remove viruses, and so on, on any of the county's equipment.

The joint library also provided wireless Internet access to patrons via the college's unfiltered wireless network. Patrons could use their own wireless laptops or borrow one from either the college or public library service desks. Lending laptops raised concerns not only about use of the unfiltered wireless network by minors but also because there were policy variations between the college and county as far as patron responsibility and charges for lost or damaged equipment. Attempts were made to find a way to operate a second wireless system by Harris County. When it was finally determined that a county-operated wireless system was not feasible, a uniform laptop checkout and damage policy was developed and approved by both entities.

RECONCILING HUMAN RESOURCE POLICIES

Because the college librarians had faculty status, each full-time librarian had a private office and telephone line. The county's human resources policy allowed only department heads to have separate offices. The remaining fifty-plus circulation and reference staff who were employed by Harris County shared three large work areas and, in some cases, shared the same cubicles and telephones. Along with work spaces, roles and responsibilities were also visibly different. College librarians spent a significant amount of time away from the reference desk and their offices because they were meeting with faculty as part of their subject liaison responsibilities, serving on hiring, accreditation, and curriculum-related committees, and participating in student activities and programs sponsored by the college. Harris County's reference librarians had more direct supervision and less independence, with specified lunch hours and assigned daily or weekly tasks to complete during their off-desk hours. The full-time college librarians worked only daytime hours, and only Monday through Friday. Adjunct librarians covered the evening and weekend shifts and the semester breaks for the college. All of the county librarians were required to cover some evening hours each week and rotating Saturday shifts and even some Sunday hours at other county library locations. All of the full-time college library employees also enjoyed a four-day workweek in the summers while the county library employees worked the same schedule year-round.

Although the administrators feared that there would be morale problems because there were dramatic differences in pay scales and working conditions between the college and the county library employees, these issues rarely surfaced. Employees took the different work areas, schedules, paid holidays, vacation time, and lunch periods in stride. A few younger employees, and those that were not already heavily invested in the retirement system, were able to advance their careers by switching to one of the higher-paying positions for the other library employer, since the college paid librarians more and the county paid more for the circulation positions.

Unexpectedly, it was the difference in payroll policies related to inclement weather that caused the most feelings of resentment and hardship for employees. The college generously paid all full-time and part-time employees when the college was closed for a few days before and after Hurricane Rita in 2005. The public library employees had to follow the county's policy and make up their hours during the same time period or lose pay or vacation time, even though they were working in a library facility that was closed by order of the college district's chancellor.

In September 2008 a much more devastating storm, Hurricane Ike, slammed the Houston area. The damage from fallen trees, flooding, and widespread power and telecommunication outages literally shut down the metropolitan area for days. It took about a week for the flooding to subside, the roads to reopen, and limited electrical power to be restored. When the Tomball College's facilities crew was able to inspect all of the buildings, they discovered significant damage due to water infiltration on both floors of the joint library facility. The college would reopen, but officials were unsure of when and if the library could reopen. The restoration consultants hired by the college said it could be several months before any employee would be allowed back into the library building to work. The mold remediation process required everyone to stay out of the library until it was completely dry, the soaked carpeting and wet sheetrock were replaced, all of the surfaces were scrubbed, and all of the library items damaged by the rains or high humidity were disposed of. Then there would still need to be extensive testing of the air quality before a decision could be made on when to reopen the library.

Only a handful of library employees had home phone or Internet access when the extended closure was announced. Those who did slowly began gathering at the Tomball campus. After making sure that all employees had been contacted, they and their families were safe, and everyone understood the situation, the next step was to brainstorm ways to reestablish essential library functions during the extended shutdown. Within two days, the library resumed limited operations in space borrowed from the student activities department in the main college campus building. Bar code scanners, laptop computers, copiers, office supplies, and chairs and tables were rounded up. The lesson learned from the earlier hurricane was that quickly finding places and projects for people to work on was critical in order to protect the paychecks of the county employees. No one wanted to see any of their colleagues' lives disrupted over three or more weeks of lost pay.

Since nothing could be handled routinely, everyone was forced to start thinking outside the box and to quickly adapt to the new environment. The children's story times were conducted in the college's theater. Library instruction sessions were demonstrated from laptops connected to the projection units in the students' regular classrooms. Face-to-face reference assistance resumed, as well as phone, chat, and e-mail consultations. Detailed information was disseminated to the college's students and anyone else who needed immediate access to library resources on how to access the online books and full-text articles. From the mounting piles of returned items, materials were redirected for library outreach programs at schools and senior centers. Quiet spaces were even found so that the college tutoring program could continue and students did not fall behind or drop their courses.

During the period the library was shut down, everyone, from the codirector to the college's work study students, volunteered for shifts at the information stations outside the library entrance and in front of the book drop. County and college library employees sat side by side in the hot sun collecting the materials users wanted to return, providing updated information on when the library would reopen and where full library services were available, and even spreading some cheer by letting people know there would be no overdue fines or replacement charges for materials damaged during the storm. Hearing directly from users how much they missed using the library and its resources built a new sense of cohesion and rallied the spirits of the staff. The weeks of working in a changed environment transformed the way the two library staffs and the learning center staff viewed and treated each other. Distinctions due to different employers, job titles, and full or part-time status vanished. Everyone felt appreciated and for the first time really part of one team. The shared hurricane recovery experience did more than any professional development exercise or cross-training event to strengthen the trust and respect among the library's employees, open up communications, and encourage innovation.

CHANGING PARTNERSHIP DYNAMICS

The creation of the joint libraries at Tomball and CyFair changed not just the way these two facilities would manage and share materials. All of the HCPL branches, the other campus and satellite libraries in the college district, and the college's long-term automation partner since 1993, the neighboring Montgomery County Memorial Library System, had to find new ways to cooperate. By the time the Tomball library was being planned, a circulation team made up of representatives of all three library systems was formed and immediately went to work to find solutions that satisfied all three partners. The first thing the circulation team did to improve customer service was to standardize the circulation periods, fines, and renewal policies so that every user was treated the same. Working out such an agreement was not easy. For instance, Harris County allowed twenty-six renewals. To alleviate the fears that Montgomery County materials could be in the hands of Harris County patrons for as long as a year, all sides agreed to a limit of two renewals and restrictions on high-demand items. Tomball and CyFair library users were often shown a complicated Venn diagram (figure 9.1) and were told that they were in the "golden egg" since they had enhanced borrowing privileges and were able to use the circulating resources of any of the five NHMCCD college campus libraries, the twenty-three branches of the Harris County Public Library, and the seven branches of NHMCCD's other consortium partner, the Montgomery County Memorial Library System.

Within months of opening the joint library at Tomball, the technical staffs for Harris County, Montgomery County, and the college district were able to merge the catalogs of all three systems and simplify the user interface. The new catalog system was even given a name that reflected their new shared vision of resource sharing, Harmonic. The unified Harmonic catalog was such a success that the college and public library partners had to quickly revise the courier's delivery routes and schedule to handle the explosive growth in the number of holds and transfers to other library locations. The circulation staffs met frequently for training on the new procedures and relied heavily on each other to resolve any issues their users faced when checking out materials, requesting items, or paying for lost or damaged items owned by another

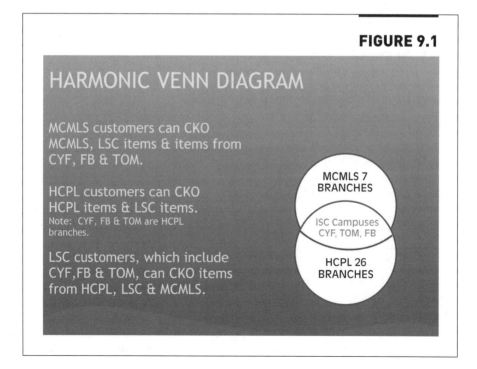

FIGURE 9.1

HARMONIC VENN DIAGRAM

MCMLS customers can CKO MCMLS, LSC items & items from CYF, FB & TOM.

HCPL customers can CKO HCPL items & LSC items.
Note: CYF, FB & TOM are HCPL branches.

LSC customers, which include CYF, FB & TOM, can CKO items from HCPL, LSC & MCMLS.

MCMLS 7 BRANCHES

ISC Campuses CYF, TOM, FB

HCPL 26 BRANCHES

partner. Users of each of the three library systems were thrilled at the wider access to materials and having new options for returning or having materials delivered to the library that was most convenient to them. The single catalog made a huge difference in the smooth operations of the joint libraries and helped the staff of all three systems see the immediate and concrete benefits for the customer that resulted from the expansion of resource-sharing efforts.

LESSONS LEARNED FROM THE FIRST FIVE YEARS

Looking back at how the joint library at Tomball developed, some things stick out as missed opportunities or unnecessary obstacles that hopefully others considering a joint library will not overlook.

Care, Feed, and Inform Stakeholders

Joint libraries require a lot of public relations time and effort to be launched and to be sustained. The key players in making the decision have to solidly support the idea and be tough enough to withstand waves of criticism. Timing of the announcement proposing a joint library also matters. Joint library negotiations are sensitive and require confidentiality as the possibility is explored, but the announcement should not take key constituencies by surprise. A joint library needs informed and committed supporters who will quickly champion the proposal. The upheaval of emotions in the Tomball community erupted from people who had founded and supported the public library for decades. These long-term supporters felt left out of the decision making and that their past efforts were devalued when the joint library was announced. College faculty and staff also felt blindsided by the announcement and were upset that the campus tradition of shared governance between college administrators and teaching faculty had been violated. To overcome this rocky start, study groups were quickly launched to counteract the hard feelings that were spreading in the community and college. Enlarging the number of participants made the process messier, but it reopened the lines of communication and proved that the college and public library system were listening to the community and the faculty. Public and academic libraries have loyal followers not only because of the depth of their collections, newest materials, or abundance of technology, but also because they create a sense of belonging and personal ownership. The faithful clientele value libraries for the same reasons portrayed in the television show *Cheers*. It is a place they love and want to preserve because everyone knows your name, the layout stays the same, and the staff does not change.

Value Insight of All Your Employees

The decision to build joint libraries is made by political leaders, governing boards, college presidents, and, hopefully, library administrators. The success of a joint library, however, is in the hands of its employees. The enthusiasm of employees is contagious, but so are their fears if they feel disenfranchised or threatened by uncertain futures. The employees have a pulse on what users like and need and can provide unique insights on what is lacking in the current facilities. Listening to these insights keeps everyone feeling that they are still on the team and strengthens the functionality of the new facility.

In the case of Tomball, there would have been more employee buy-in and less suspicion of what the other side was up to if the planning and design of the new library had been a more open and inclusive process. There was an urgency to get the revised building plans finalized quickly while the capital funds were still available for the project and before more turmoil erupted. It was difficult for the employees to embrace the new library when they were kept out of the picture and hidden away from their new colleagues. The lack of input from the employees who would actually interact with the users and each other in the new facility meant the layout was not as efficient or as flexible for future needs. There were numerous items that the design teams overlooked but would have been on employees' wish lists and could have been modified without significant increase in costs, such as:

- additional electrical outlets (for patron laptops, phone chargers, staff areas, maintenance equipment, self-checkout stations)
- more visible locations for public restrooms, copy rooms, and print stations
- soundproofing in the group study rooms, tutoring areas, and young adult room
- work areas that allowed for an increased number of employees and growth in circulation
- expandable shelving areas
- appropriately sized book display units for preschoolers
- more attention to the security needs for the buildings (public address system, location of security gates, controlled entrances to the main campus)

Separate, but Not Equal

Before opting for separate employers in a joint library, all of the immediate and long-term ramifications of that decision, on existing and future employees, need to be analyzed. Creating a seamless joint library is much more difficult when you have two employers with different procedures, forms, benefits, dress codes, time-sheet deadlines, network log-ins, evaluation systems, pay scales, retirement plans, e-mail, vacation plans, and support for professional development. At Tomball a single employer was not chosen because there were real concerns that long-term employees would be negatively affected at retirement or would be forced to choose employment elsewhere in the system in order to retain their years of service. If Lone Star College had been named the employer, the college district's nonparticipation in Social Security would have triggered the Social Security Administration's complicated government offset and windfall provisions, resulting in reduced benefits at retirement and possible loss of higher spousal benefits for the transferred public library employees. If the county had been named the employer, all of the college employees would have faced significant reductions in vacation/holiday benefits. On county pay scales, the college support staff would have enjoyed moderate increases, but the college's librarians would have faced much lower pay scales and loss of faculty status. With a single employer, each partner also would have had to face dealing with the impact of higher pay scales on annual operating budgets and maintaining equity among employees at other locations within its larger system.

Invest in Your New Team

The delay in appointing the two codirectors at Tomball to just a couple of months before the new library opened meant that the leadership was, as one would expect, consumed with the physical logistics of the move and the preparations for the opening day celebration. Investing time, energy, and attention to creating a cohesive working team ended up on the back burner. Instead of revamping procedures and creating new routines that best suited the partnership, each side arrived and immediately began operating with its own traditions and according to its own agenda. Instead of seeing the joint library as a new planet and encouraging exploration and innovation, each side staked out its territory and politely stayed within its boundaries. There were no incentives for employees to investigate new ways of doing things or opportunities for the staff to get to know each other before the trucks with the library materials arrived and each side rushed to get their items on their shelves and in order before the doors officially opened. Greater interaction between the two staffs before the joint library opened would have enhanced a sense of trust and cooperation. It was counterproductive not to know everyone's name, who was bilingual, or at least to know who had subject expertise in a certain area.

As soon as a joint library is announced, steps need to be taken to start developing a new culture and delegate some of the decision making. At Tomball there was a significant overlap in reference holdings. The review of reference materials would have been a neutral place to start discussions among the two sets of librarians hired to work in the new library. It would have been a good way to start changing perspectives on who would be served in the new library, identify any unmet needs, collaborate on what to do with duplicates, and then designate funds for joint purchases. Having opportunities to work side by side wears down the suspicion and resistance to change, and eases the need for competition.

Friction is inevitable in any newly "blended family." Everyone feels uncertain and a degree of discomfort and resentment toward the new parents and siblings when two or more libraries marry. Empowering employees to find the solutions gives them a goal that they invest in instead of spending their time absorbed in cataloging the other partner's perceived defects or working behind the scenes to make the marriage fail. The two codirectors were hampered in their efforts to quickly implement a plan for real team building because they themselves were still exploring and observing the other's communication and management style.

At Tomball there were numerous "all staff meetings" with top-down directives and visits from upper managements sharing platitudes about working together, but very limited opportunities to let the staff identify issues and concerns and solve the problems they encountered. Small self-managed teams with representation from both partners would have increased the cross-fertilization of ideas and removed some of the feelings of "us against them." There were many events that gave the appearance of uniting the two staffs, such as when the codirectors scheduled combined staff circulation and reference meetings. Unfortunately, these "all staff" gatherings did not energize the staff or stimulate new ideas because too often they followed the "members only meeting" each codirector had held a day or two earlier with her own employees that subtly reemphasized the traditional boundaries for each group and reinforced the idea that unilateral strategies were preferred.

Make Technology Work for You

The information technology and library technical systems personnel need to be pivotal players on the facility and long-term planning teams for a joint library. It is one thing to support a library with a few dozen computers, and quite another to open a new facility with hundreds of computers on two different networks with different patron authentication protocols. For users to have smooth and easy access to the growing assortment of online resources, it is imperative to keep the tech gurus in the loop.

The Tomball joint library presented an array of challenges to the technical support and IT staffs at both institutions. Some challenges they welcomed because they love to try new things, test new equipment, and bat around ideas with peers at other institutions and with knowledgeable vendors. Other challenges made them cringe because they knew the current systems were inadequate for the new demand and they were more aware than others that the long-term solutions would not be fast, cheap, or easy to implement.

Joint libraries can dramatically change the operating rhythms or established work cycles for the partnering institutions. The college system had routinely used winter and spring breaks to upgrade software, install new servers, and test new programs. Once the college system joined with the county libraries, the opportunities for scheduled downtime periods shrank dramatically. What had traditionally been the college's slow times were the public library's peak times—summer reading programs, for example. Both parties were forced to think differently on how the systems operated and what support they needed. The merged Harmonic catalog made circulation more efficient and easier for patrons to place holds on materials, but secondarily it improved the collection development policies of all the parties and forced the standardization of catalog entries and holdings information. The shared catalog meant there was less duplication of materials, a wider awareness of what was on order, and more professional eyes spotting where there were gaps in the collection and noticing items that were outdated and needed to be replaced or withdrawn.

A JOINT LIBRARY NEEDS A NEW PARADIGM

It is well known that standards and uniform procedures make large institutions run smoothly. But it is also well known that just because something has been done a certain way for a long time, it does not mean that it is still the best way or will work in a new environment. Joint libraries, especially those with dual employers, need permission to be flexible and allowed exceptions from their administrative systems on how to operate. One of the most powerful exceptions made at Tomball was that the fine money collected no longer had to be given back to the institution. An allocation formula for the fine money was determined based on past circulation patterns for the college and county library branch. Allowing the fine money to be kept by the library meant that the codirectors could use the funds for staff professional development, guest speakers and supplies for special programming, marketing the library with banners and giveaways, and joint purchases of materials or equipment.

Despite all of these differences and the ongoing backroom debates on how to operate, what began as the Tomball College and Community Library and is today known as the Lone Star College-Tomball Community Library was and is a successful joint library. To be honest, there was considerable trepidation when the building opened that even peaceful coexistence might be too lofty a goal. The lengthy negotiations had bruised and battered all of the internal players involved. There was an unhealthy focus on what would stay segregated and protecting one side's territory from the other's control. The joint library's success at Tomball was due not to an administrative mandate or to the ability of the two codirectors to work out their differences; the success occurred because the personnel on the service desks and the technical staffs truly wanted to provide the best customer service to all of its users. It was their enthusiasm, willingness to take a risk, and persistence in finding better ways to make things happen that has earned the library the respect and support it now enjoys.

CASE STUDY
University Branch–Sugar Land, Fort Bend County Library, Texas. University of Houston–Sugar Land and the Wharton County Junior College

In the development of the Fort Bend University Branch library, the agreement between the Fort Bend Public Libraries and the University of Houston (UH) developed because it was advantageous to both sides. UH had the land on their campus for a library, but not necessarily the available funding to build a new facility. The Fort Bend Public Libraries had money for construction but did not want to spend that money in acquiring land. An initial agreement for the library was made between the two entities as well as Wharton County Junior College (WCJC). However, Fort Bend had previously tried to develop a process with the Fort Bend Independent School District to use a school library after school hours as a public library, but that arrangement had fallen apart. What made this partnership come to fruition?

Fort Bend Commissioner James Patterson called a meeting of the librarians involved (James Patterson, pers. comm.). As he tells it, once he got everyone together in the same room, he told them to uncross their arms. This is an excellent metaphor for the process of getting people to set aside their natural

University Branch, exterior view from plaza. Rendering by Bailey Architects.

concerns about how this is going to affect them and their library and begin the planning for a new endeavor without a sense of territory. Patterson wanted the new library to have no sense of "this is my library" from one side and "this is my library" from the other. The development of the joint agreement took about four months while the overall planning of the space took approximately eighteen months. Jamie Knight, architect, commented that he thought there were many "mental barriers" that needed to be overcome before the process came together (Jamie Knight, pers. comm.).

Having one entity in charge of the library is listed as a factor for the success of a joint library by Haycock, although there are successful outliers to this rule (2006). The model selected for the University Branch of the Fort Bend County Library, which opened in the fall of 2011, is to have the library run by the public partner, with UH providing funding. Additionally, WCJC has contracted with UH to have a partnership in the library. This model was chosen because the University of Houston Library dean Dana Rook did not want to run a library which had two types of librarians: academic and public. She saw too many obstacles (Dana Rook, pers. comm.). For one, she did not want the university to have to deal with censorship if a community patron wanted to have a book removed from the collection. She also did not want to be in charge of a library which practiced filtering of computer content. She notified the current academic librarians on the campus that the new library would be a public library, hiring public librarians. If they wanted to continue working at the library, they had to apply just like any other prospective librarian. Certainly this library will be a bigger and better library than any one entity could create by itself. But essentially it is a big public library being built on a college campus, being run by the county of Fort Bend. College librarians and administrators must wonder what the impact on accreditation this may have in the future.

COLLECTION

The library collection is being developed by Fort Bend County as they would for any new branch. The collection development librarian is working with library vendors, but has not had specific requests from the UH campus. WCJC is providing library materials that will be cataloged and added to the library collection. For UH students, faculty will still be able to put their personal items on reserve for students' use in the library. Students will be able to request materials from other Fort Bend libraries, as well as pick up materials requested from other UH system libraries.

As for database access, only the public library's databases will be available to all users. UH and WCJC students must use their student identification cards to use the university and college databases respectively. All computers will be public library computers with access through Fort Bend's T1 lines.

There will be a university liaison librarian who will coordinate teaching database instruction classes and providing library orientations for WCJC students and (to a lesser extent) UH. This librarian will have the same qualifications as all public librarians, but Clara Russell, director of Fort Bend County Public Libraries, said that teaching experience would be a plus (Clara Russell, pers. comm.). Although the library will have a computer lab, it is expected that classes for students will be held in the students' regular classroom or other college/university computer labs. The classes themselves will not be taught by designated librarians but by all adult services librarians. The current job description has the expectation that librarians will be able to teach computer and other classes for the public, and it is assumed that they will also be able to meet the academic library instruction needs.

IS THIS MODEL AN ANOMALY OR A TREND?

By not hiring the academic librarians already on the University of Houston staff, Fort Bend greatly simplified its personnel issues. Everyone is aware up front that this library is primarily a big public library that serves the needs of the university and college for a fee. If North Lake Community Library had been up front like this, their joint library still might exist. The myriad nuances of a truly blended library are missing in this partnership arrangement, but is representative of a growing trend of libraries adopting a fee-based model to serve multiple constituencies.

▆▆▆▆▆▆▆▆

CASE STUDY
North Lake Community Library

A Joint Project between the City of Irving, Texas, and North Lake College, Irving, Texas, Part of the Dallas County Community College District

After a long board meeting of the Irving Public Library, two board members struck up a conversation one late afternoon in the mid-1990s. Lamar Veatch, director of the Irving Public Library since the early 1980s, and Jim Horton, president of North Lake College (1982–96), were friends and colleagues who brainstormed an idea: why not join forces and create a library both for the public and for the faculty and student body of North Lake College? According to Patty Landers Caperton, former director of communications at the Irving Public Library, these two charismatic leaders took their passion and forged a partnership at the highest level to create a library they envisioned as being greater than the sum of its parts (Patty Caperton, pers.comm.). They saw a way to share resources, open an academic door to the community, and enhance student learning with an improved research facility. President Jim Horton also was looking for a way to lower processing costs for each book in the college library. The city had the money to invest in infrastructure. The college would gain a financial advantage with the city's deeper pockets. Their vision was infectious, and leaders from both the public library and the college came on board. The college would build the library structure, and the public library would purchase equipment, furniture, and books. There would be a shared, but separate staff. Money was to be saved with the shared processing of materials. On June 18, 1998, a contract was signed. One of the provisions was that it was to be reevaluated every six years (See appendixes B and C for a copy.)

COLLEGE INPUT

When the partnership was formed, the head librarian of North Lake College, Enrique Chamberlain, was not convinced that this arrangement would actually benefit the college community (Enrique Chamberlain, pers. comm.). Chamberlain, a well-respected faculty member of the college since it opened in1977, had a substantial amount of political capital at the grassroots level in the college. He was not offered the position of branch manager. In fact, he was moved from the library to a position elsewhere in the college. He continued to have an influence in the college as many colleagues and students would consult him rather than the librarians in the joint library.

NATATORIUM MODEL: FATAL FLAW?

Years before this partnership, President Jim Horton had approached the city to build a pool which the college could jointly use with the city. President Horton saw this endeavor as a means to outsource the pool to the city, which knew how to run and operate a public pool. With some shared capital as an investment, the college would have use of this public facility. This worked beautifully for the natatorium (James Horton, pers. comm.). But when it was chosen as the model for the joint library, questions arose. Essentially this model would make the library a public facility, run by the public library, not by the college. The faculty saw the library for what it was: a public library and not an integral part of the college (Enrique Chamberlain, pers. comm.). Small obstacles were thrown at the college faculty when they tried to use library services. For example, the public librarians required faculty to schedule bibliographic instruction classes two weeks in advance. They even tried to offer generic instruction classes rather than classes geared to an assignment or a discipline. Students also were allotted a finite time on the computers. This created a hardship on the students and faculty who wanted and needed research instruction and research time on the computers. The city allotted $1 million for books and materials, $200,000 of which could be selected by college librarians. President Horton wanted a top-notch library that would serve the neighboring Las Colinas master-planned community, which is populated with many prominent corporations. He also knew that this proposed library was popular with the public and would help to sell the bond issue (which it did) (James Horton, pers. comm.).

LIBRARY MANAGEMENT

Who would be chosen as the branch manager of the library? An academic librarian or a public librarian? Who had the primary hiring authority? A decision was made by the Irving Public Library to put one of its current librarians in the position. Lyle Vance had a Ph.D. and was presumed to be well qualified to run both a public and a college library.

This decision may be perceived as a proverbial line in the sand. While some academic librarians from the college still worked in the new library, right from the beginning the public library was making the decisions and leading the venture. The college did have input (no reserved parking for the public; security tags for books; Library of Congress classification), but was never truly an equal in the partnership. James Karney, former assistant director of the Irving Public Library, notes ironically that the public library felt that North Lake had too much say in the relationship (James Karney, pers. comm.). Roles and expectations were not adequately spelled out in the contract. The contract did say the public library would run the day-to-day operations, but reporting lines remained vague.

LEADERSHIP CHANGES

By 1999 both Veatch and Horton had moved on in their careers, the former taking a position as the director of libraries for the state of Georgia and the latter as chancellor of San Jacinto College in Houston. It would be up to the subsequent leaders to implement this partnership. While it was believed to be a great boon for the public and college, the partnership now had none of the originators on board. The city manager hired Nancy Smith in 1999 as the director of the Irving Public Library. She was told that she needed to try to make it work since it was an inherited obligation (Nancy Smith, pers. comm.). This was not an auspicious directive for a director who would be required to oversee the construction and fruition of the endeavor. In fact, she left for Kings County in Seattle in 2002, just after the library opened. Although North Lake College Community Library held a grand and exciting opening with James Earl Jones delivering an inspirational speech about the power of education, the excitement and vision could not be sustained.

CONTRACT

The simplest way to divide up the obligations was to have the college build the building and have the public library furnish it, including the collection materials. With little commingling of funds, the simplicity of the agreement perhaps foreshadowed the eventual split. The college community felt an absence of faith in the de facto public library. Even though all the librarians were performing both public and academic library activities, including bibliographic instruction to the students, there was an undercurrent in the college community that the academic side had been given short shrift. When the accreditation agency SACS visited the college, they interviewed the faculty and student body. This was a way for the undercurrent to become palpable and vocal. The partnership which was never really a partnership was unraveling. The library opened in September 2002 and it would end just two years later.

The public library equally had its doubts. The economy was suffering post-9/11 woes. The city was putting a lot of money into the project without large numbers of patrons (except for the hugely successful children's library). It is not understood why the public did not flock to this new library. Perhaps it was the demographics. The Las Colinas area was very upscale, but the college's student body came from a lower socioeconomic level (Lamar Veatch, pers. comm.). The corporate clientele Horton wished for never materialized.

The six-year mark came in 2004 and the contract was up for review. All parties needed to examine how the partnership was going. There was no longer a clear impetus for continuing the relationship. Every six years they were to evaluate the partnership to see if it were to remain. "One thing we didn't talk about that may be noteworthy—we just didn't decide one day to end the partnership. On the city's side, the city manager, City Council, and Library Advisory Board were all in agreement about ending the partnership. Dr. Herlinda Glasscock, the new president of North Lake College, was an outstanding, wonderful leader who was a gracious negotiator and agreed with Irving to end the partnership" (Patty Caperton, pers. comm.).

The two cultures never coalesced and the contract was written such that there was an easy way out. The college kept the building, and the public library had everything else.

The breakup was actually a catalyst for something better. A new 59,000-square-foot college library was built that was so beautiful it made the cover of *Choice* in September 2008 (Enrique Chamberlain, pers. comm.). The public library built a 25,000-square-foot facility called the Valley Ranch Library.

The sides parted amicably and life went on. Lamar Veatch, whose leadership brought about this project, reflects on this outcome. "There were no bad guys" (Lamar Veatch, pers. comm.). The joint endeavor, in fact, put both entities in a better place. There is no easy blueprint for success since there are so many factors. Enthusiasm must come from top management and be embraced by the worker bees. "Maybe we did give the college library short shrift." Maybe the college leadership should have invested more effort in bringing the librarians and faculty on board with the idea. "People are down on what they are not up on."

CASE STUDY
Virginia Beach Joint-Use Library

A Joint Project between the Tidewater Community
College and the City of Virginia Beach

Around 2003, the city of Virginia Beach was planning an 18,000-square-foot library across from the Tidewater Community College. Tidewater Virginia Beach campus was planning a 100,000-square-foot Learning Resources Center with a 50,000-square-foot addition in the future (Garrow 2005, V3). When the college president, Deborah DiCroce, and the city manager, Jim Spore, discovered these seemingly redundant plans, the city and college began discussing pooling of resources to make an even better library. The college is a state-supported institution and the public library a city-supported institution. Combining these two disparate entities to create one seamless library seemed daunting indeed. Two separate payrolls in one institution is the model for San Jose State University's and the City of San Jose's Martin Luther King, Jr. Library, a success story of shared dreams and captured reality.

Virginia Beach Joint-Use Library, exterior entrance. Rendering by RRMM.

FEASIBILITY STUDY

A feasibility study was conducted by California-based Anderson Brulé Architects after intense focus groups, visits to each other's facilities, and a two-day workshop held in August 2005 (Garrow 2005, V3).

Anderson Brulé had experience with joint public/academic libraries as the architectural consultant for the San Jose project. "Their sense of 'what' was feasible was to dream bigger and larger than any precedent for joint use and to craft the 'community empowering vision' that was created in the session referred to in the workshop as MTL—'More than a Library'" (Anderson Brulé 2005, 3).

When this dedicated grassroots group of about sixty college and city officials, library staff, students, faculty, and residents finished their workshop, it was agreed that the project was definitely worth pursuing. They realized that it would not save much money, but two entities could create a facility so much better than doing so alone. The November 4, 2005, study was placed online and the excitement and collaborative spirit infused every page.

CHALLENGES

There are always obstacles to creating something different, and the team tried to identify some perceived challenges to this endeavor. "Whether real or imagined, the cultures of the two organizations are perceived as different" (Anderson Brulé 2005, 3). Are the missions and service philosophies so different that one or both would be compromised? Would there be competition for resources? Would faculty have access to academic sources for their research? Would the public be intimidated by a library on a college campus? How would the operation and facilities management work? Who pays for the custodian? Are spaces restricted to any groups of users? Dewey or Library of Congress? Different compensation models and benefit systems can cause a perception of unfairness and discord. Can staff, leadership, and stakeholders remain collaborative and not competitive? (Anderson Brulé, 2005, 3).

DECISIONS MADE

As of September 2011, some decisions have been made about this future library. Mary Mayer-Hennelly, associate vice president for learning resources at Tidewater Community College, spoke about these decisions.

The name of the future library changed from the Virginia Beach Lifelong Learning Center to Virginia Beach Joint-Use Library. The name changed again: Tidewater Community College Virginia Beach Campus Joint-Use Library. The name may change in the future. There will be one director who will be an academic librarian and paid by the college (Mary Mayer-Hennelly, pers. comm.). John Massey of Tidewater's facilities planning development notes that since the college pays 83 percent of the cost, they have a majority rule, so to speak, and thus a director will be hired by the college with academic credentials. Other staff will be from both entities and probably will be paid by their respective parties. Academic librarians will do all the bibliographic instruction, but the reference desk will be staffed by both types of librarians. There will be seamless service and no "us and them" mentality and all spaces will be shared, unlike San Jose where different collections are housed on different floors (John Massey, pers. comm.).

The community colleges in Virginia are state-funded (rather than locally controlled and predominantly locally funded like Lone Star College). All of the community colleges in the state share the same catalog system which is run out of Richmond, the state capital. The catalogs will be searchable by using Ex Libris's Metalib, a federated search engine capable of combining searches on both catalogs. The majority of the community colleges' online databases are from VIVA (the Virginia higher education consortium for online resource sharing and interlibrary loan). The public libraries, on the other hand, have online access to databases separately through the state library. Gene Damon, director of library automation for the Virginia Community College System, said that access to databases on-site will be available to all users, but each entity only has remote access to its own databases. It would be prohibitively costly to combine remote access because database companies base price on the size of the user population (Gene Damon, pers. comm.).

The Dewey Decimal Classification System will be used for the children's nonfiction collection and the fiction collections will be arranged alphabetically by author. The adult nonfiction will be classified using Library of Congress. There will be no filtering of computers except in the children's room (John Massey, pers. comm.).

PREDICTORS OF SUCCESS

We thought it would be interesting to follow the development of this work in progress and speculate as to whether it will be a success. Ken Haycock of the San Jose State University School of Library Science wrote an article in 2006 on guidelines for the success of dual-use libraries and said: "From the work of researchers in three countries, predictors of success can be articulated" (488).

The ten criteria:

1. The population of the community to be served is less than 10,000.
2. A formal planning process involving the significant stakeholders will be undertaken. Community involvement and support will be evident.
3. There will be a written legal agreement for governance, administration, finances, and operations. Guidelines for evaluation and dissolution will be included.
4. A single, independent, representative decision-making board or management committee will develop policies and procedures and engage and evaluate the director.
5. An integrated facility (not two libraries sharing one facility) is preferred; the facility will be conveniently and visibly located and large enough to accommodate a variety of groups and resources. A separate area for adults and designated parking will be provided.
6. The library will be connected with a larger network, regional system, or consortium.
7. The principal of the school should have a strong desire for success, and teachers should support the concept; support for the integrated service will be a specific factor in hiring and transfer decisions.

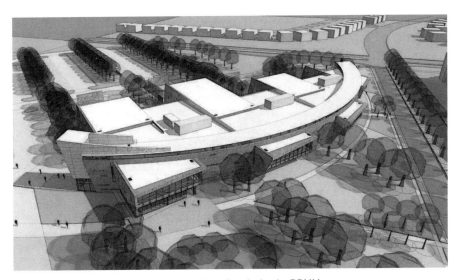

Virginia Beach Joint-Use Library, aerial view. Rendering by RRMM.

8. One highly motivated professional librarian will be in charge and report to a single governance board.
9. There will be regular discussion of effective communication at all levels and planned cooperation between public library staff and school staff.
10. There will be no restrictions on access to print, audio/video, or electronic resources or on the circulation of materials. (492–93)

The authors of this book have developed their own revised list of criteria for joint library success:

1. Buy-in from all constituencies; there must be financial incentives for both sides.
2. Formal planning process
3. Written agreement
4. Visible presence in community/good location
5. Either one director or two directors who are committed to the collaboration
6. Seamless service; merged collections; no territoriality
7. Preferred one payroll
8. True collaboration, not just one entity running the facility
9. Libraries have to embrace and invest in innovation to succeed.

Virginia Beach Joint-Use Library, north courtyard. Rendering by RRMM.

KEY COMPONENTS

The college and city hired a consultant, Anderson Brulé Architects, to facilitate talks between the parties and other stakeholders. Pamela Anderson-Brulé states, "The company's longer-term goal is to move beyond designing buildings and into designing 'cultural systems.'" She cites San Jose's Dr. Martin Luther King, Jr. Library as one example of a cultural system within a building. The San Jose Public Library and SJSU needed first to decide how to work together before the designs for the building could be finished. Pamela Anderson-Brulé said that more organizations are recognizing that they need a partner to survive and that it ultimately affects the space that's designed ("Anderson Brulé Architects" 2010). The Virginia project relied heavily on the planning process that Anderson Brulé put into place. They used San Jose as a model, but differed in some of their decisions. They probably will have two payrolls, but only one director, who is an academic librarian. As mentioned above, the college will provide the leadership since it is funding 83 percent of the bill. At San Jose, there is more of a 50/50 partnership. Most of the space in the Virginia Beach library will be shared, unlike at San Jose where different floors are designated for public and university use and some university collections and databases are restricted. As in San Jose, academic librarians will do the bibliographic instruction, but both academic and public librarians will work side by side at the reference desk. Initially at San Jose a tiered reference system was used, and the academic librarians were not expected to work at the reference desk. Instead, they concentrated on teaching library research and purchasing curriculum-specific materials, and handled advanced reference questions by referral. After layoffs, they do not have the level of staffing needed to do that in its pure form and so the university librarians spend some time on the desk and also receive referrals, Dean Kifer explains (Ruth Kifer, pers. comm.).

PREDICTIONS

Let's look at our criteria for success and see if the Virginia Beach Campus Joint-Use Library will succeed:

1. Buy-in from All Constituencies

President Deborah DiCroce and City Manager James Spore came up with the joint-use idea and were passionate about shepherding the partnership during its formative years. The workshop in 2005 under the leadership of Anderson

Brulé Architects adroitly included all kinds of stakeholders: city officials, library staff, students, faculty, and residents. In the short term, having a large group of grassroots stakeholders created an immediate, positive, and optimistic response about this "More than a Library" concept and, in the long term, will continue to be used as an avenue to spread the word about the benefits and milestones for the joint library throughout the community.

2. Formal Planning Process

Anderson Brulé Architects did most of the planning initially with the help of constituents in the 2005 workshop. Hiring outside experts in the joint concept is a good start to success because they can facilitate an open dialogue.

3. Written Agreement

As of September 2011, a memorandum of understanding was in process and moving along well (John Massey, pers. comm.). The agreement needs to be finalized and ratified by both parties before the library is opened. Rebecca Dames was hired in February 2012 as director of the joint-use library. She previously worked as the library services coordinator at Northern Arizona University.

4. Visible Presence in the Community/Good Location

The library will be on the Tidewater Campus. The design is for a large and beautiful facility.

5. Either One or Two Directors Who Are Committed to the Plan

The decision to have one director will be a positive factor in the future library's success, and it is advantageous to be able to unite the staff under one leader instead of competing leaders reporting to different institutions. It will be important to hire someone who is evenhanded and will consider both constituencies.

6. Seamless Service

One of the main goals of this project is to make the public and college materials, staffing, and spaces available to all. There will be one collection with no restrictions on borrowing. Public and college librarians will work side by side. One caveat: only the academic librarians will conduct library instruction for the college. Assigning responsibilities to just one of the parties has the potential for creating feelings of inequality (or superiority) among the two groups of librarians. The library catalogs will be searchable using one interface. The databases will be shared on-site, but not remotely. Will there be a single library web page? In its commitment to erasing distinctions between the two libraries, the public library and university started out with a consolidated web page for the Dr. Martin Luther King, Jr. Library in San Jose. Patrons, however, found it complicated to navigate and frustrating to use because of remote access restrictions to university databases. A decision was made that users would be better served with two separate web pages, so a new website was launched in November 2010 with an opening page that let users immediately choose to access the public library's resources or the university's. As seen in the San Jose experience, having access to resources of multiple library systems is great, but the depth of information on how to use and who can access the resources can also hinder their use.

7. Preferred One Payroll

As it is now being planned, there will probably be two payrolls. Since the college is paying 83 percent of the cost of the library, it would make more sense to have the college hire the employees and have the city pay a bill to cover its share. There are pitfalls to having two sets of employees reporting to separate entities. The one director may ameliorate this situation, though. Joe Dahlstrom, the director of the Victoria College/University of Houston-Victoria joint use library, has two sets of employees with different pay scales and vacations and even hours worked per week. In his opinion: "Actually, if I were starting fresh, I would probably have one institution run the library with a contract to serve the other institution. With one set of employees it would simplify matters. The director would report to one boss" (Joe Dahlstrom, pers. comm.).

8. True Collaboration, Not Just One Entity Running the Facility

Right from the beginning, the college is paying 83 percent of the bill and thus is granted a leadership role. It remains to be seen if the public side is given short shrift. Although the director will be an academic librarian, it is to be hoped that this individual can balance the needs of the community with the needs of the college.

9. Innovation

Creativity and vision are important factors in the success of a joint endeavor. The online materials speak for themselves. These planners dream big and are looking for "More Than a Library."

SUCCEED?

This proposed library has incorporated most of the predictors for success. Construction is under way and on schedule, and as of September 2011, they have the equipment and book budgets, and funding is in place for staff. The library is slated to open sometime in the first half of 2013. The facilities director for the college, John Massey, writes:

> From my perspective, this is a success waiting to happen. The design is outstanding, construction is on schedule and going well, equipment budgets appear to be sized just right, the memorandum of understanding is well underway, the partners are working together well, and folks are getting excited. Seeing steel coming out of the ground always gets folks excited because it is the first evidence the hard work of the last several years is becoming a reality. (John Massey, pers. comm.)

If the idea of a bigger, better, and different library is worth anything, this joint library will be built and will thrive.

TEN

CONCLUSION

If you want to be incrementally better: Be competitive.
If you want to be exponentially better: Be cooperative.

—Unknown source.

ARE PARTNERSHIPS A TREND OF THE FUTURE?

Joint-use libraries will become more common in the twenty-first century. They make sense, have the capacity to give better service, and can provide more resources than an individual library can provide by itself. Overcoming self-interest, anxiety, fear of the unknown, and reluctance to engage in transformational thinking will be the major challenges facing shared facilities (Riggs 2000, 5).

Then again, it is possible that joint libraries are a mere blip on the radar screen of library history. The percentage of multi-jurisdictional libraries in the United States has stayed essentially constant from 2002 to 2008, with 3.5 percent in 2002 and 3.4 percent in 2008. Multi-jurisdictional libraries are those where at least one of the entities is a public library, but it excludes city/county joint libraries and college/university/community college joint ventures (Henderson, et al. 2011).

We started out this book with the idea that partnerships were the wave of the future. We believed that with technology changing so rapidly and with scarcity of funding, partnerships would be a logical step in the evolution of libraries. California and Florida are states where a growing number of libraries are joint endeavors. However, after talking to many players in joint libraries, some of us have come to the conclusion that it takes a rare combination of qualities to create and make work a true joint endeavor. One predictor of success is creativity and vision. This quality cannot be manufactured. Rare indeed are the leaders who can overcome fear of the unknown and "engage in transformational thinking" (Riggs 2000, 5). In business, partnerships are the most difficult type of business to make succeed. Even best friends who form partnerships are at risk of dissolving the agreements when self-interest and conflict arise. The usual chain of command in a typical corporation is simpler and less fraught with danger. However, when a Ben and Jerry or a Fred and Ginger can make it work, it is a beautiful thing to behold.

STRAINS ON RELATIONSHIP WHEN MONEY IS TIGHT

Many joint projects developed when times were booming, when there was extra money and optimism for creative ventures. What happens when budgets are cut? Just as individual relationships may be strained by financial woes, joint libraries too may feel the pinch and may no longer be able to meet the financial obligations required by the partnership. Conversely, the collaborative programs and abundant resources of the joint library make it a dynamic showplace. If a system needs to keep only one library open it seems to make sense that it would be the one with the most community engagement.

North Lake Community Library

The North Lake College and Irving Public Library project comes to mind. When the project was proposed by the head of the public library and the president of the college, the City of Irving was flush with funds and looking to improve library services for both the college and the community. The proposed library was on the North Lake College campus in the northern area of the city, Las Colinas, where there are prosperous corporations and wealthy suburbs. It took many years for the project to be completed and when the joint library opened, the financial climate changed dramatically downward. Both parties no longer saw a positive economic value in the relationship. Whereas once the city of Irving had deep pockets and felt that money put into the project would serve the community, in reality, the public just did not flock to the library as anticipated. As money dried up, the city reevaluated the commitment and came up short. The contract between the city of Irving and the North Lake

Community College signed in 1998 included a provision to have the agreement reviewed and renewed every six years. After only two years of operation, this agreement was up for review in 2004. According to Lyle Vance, former library manager, a perfect storm of events led the parties to decide they did not want to continue the relationship (Lyle Vance, pers. comm.). The college community felt that the joint library was shortchanging the students and faculty because it was in essence a public library, not a true partnership. Worries about accreditation loomed when the accrediting review team from SACS visited. Faculty and students complained of reduced bibliographic instruction, limited computer usage for students, and the lack of academic librarians. While these concerns did not reflect finances, the added financial strains probably contributed to the breakup. Happily, the city ended up building a showplace of a new library and the college built a new 59,000-square-foot library which ended up on the cover of *Choice* in September 2008.

Broward County

In 2007, a dispute over money arose between Broward County and Nova Southeastern University over their joint library, the Alvin Sherman Library on the Davie campus of NSU. "Broward County contributed about $31 million to the library's construction and pays a portion of annual operating costs based on how many county residents use it" (Sherman 2007). Because of the economic downturn, the county commissioners had slashed the library budget, which led to reduced hours and layoffs throughout the public library system. They also wanted a reduction in the amount they paid NSU for the annual operation of the Sherman Library. NSU instead asked Broward County to pay over $900,000 more based on its usage study. The proposed increase infuriated the county commissioners, who threatened to walk away from the library partnership. The county auditor conducted its own usage study and a compromise was negotiated. "Julie Spechler, director of public affairs at NSU, confirmed that the deal would extend to NSU the same nine percent cut the Broward County Libraries are taking. That cut alone translates into $422,712 in savings for the county" (Albanese 2007). The original contract was forty years long and there are thirty years to go. Basing the distribution of annual operating costs on usage figures was intended to be an objective method of being fair to both parties while allowing for fluctuations and changes in usage patterns over the long term of the contract. Although the contract between the county and the university was thorough and over fifty pages long, it lacked details on how NSU would track usage. This monetary dispute could have caused the demise of the joint library if cooler heads had not prevailed, and the dispute serves as a warning to other joint libraries that explicit details are needed in their agreements for defining how and when there will be adjustments to the funding formula.

Lone Star College-CyFair

Lone Star College-CyFair Branch Library of the Harris County Public Library has a different kind of agreement. Instead of reviewing the contract every six or so years as with Irving and instead of counting usage, their agreement states that the partnership will remain unless the county fails to pay the agreed amount of money. The full agreement is in appendix A.

> At such time as the County fails to exercise any of its options to pay the District the funds as provided for under Paragraphs IV or V, the sole and exclusive remedy of the District is to terminate this agreement by providing thirty days advance notice of termination to the County. (quote from appendix A)

The county pays a bill to the college in installments. If the county chooses to not pay the bill, the partnership in essence would dissolve. As of September 2011, both the college and especially the county are in a tight budgetary place. Falling real estate values have decimated the tax base and millions of dollars are being cut. The Harris County Public Library laid off eight full-time employees, has shortened hours significantly, is contemplating possible closings of branches, and due to a hiring freeze has over 15 percent of its positions unfilled. Some limited hiring has taken place, but the staff is inadequate to resume normal hours and services. At CyFair, one of the three largest libraries in the 25-branch system, if layoffs are required, the nature of the agreement will have to be changed. The positions in the joint library are funded in different ways. For example, the children's librarians are funded 100 percent by the county. The reference librarians are mostly funded by the college with some 70/30 and some 50/50 (as is the director and assistant director). If layoffs are necessary, this very well could constitute a breach of the agreement. Thus, it can be hoped that this branch will survive the draconian cuts coming up. However, HCPL is pleased with the joint libraries and has not indicated any intent to make changes. These libraries are some of the showcases of the system.

Dr. Martin Luther King, Jr. Library

The Dr. Martin Luther King, Jr. Library in California, which is a joint project between San Jose State University and the San Jose Public Library, has faced huge budget cuts. Since this library has two payrolls and two directors, the layoffs they experienced are from both the city and the university. The dean of libraries, Ruth Kifer, reports that formerly the university librarians did not have to work the reference desk, but after the layoffs, they now are on the desk. They also now are closing the library at 9 p.m. instead of 10 p.m. to save money. The public is asked to leave while students may stay until midnight, since student fees support keeping the library open for them only (Ruth Kifer, pers. comm.).

Since the public library is contractually committed to certain levels of spending at the MLK library, this does leave them with less money for other branches. However, the decision to keep the main library more fully funded might have happened anyway since it is the main library and the dynamic effects of the joint library make it the heart of the system. If a system needs to keep only one library open it seems to make sense that it would be the one with the most community engagement.

Lone Star College-Tomball Community Library

Similarly, Lone Star College-Tomball Community Library, a branch of the Harris County Public Library, has two staffs and two codirectors. Their agreement would allow the college and county to lay off employees in each respective staff without renegotiating the agreement. In fact, the public library, which started out with 60 employees when it opened in January 2005, as of early 2011 had 40 employees and expects to lose more as staff are reassigned to smaller branches facing a critical number of vacancies.

Tidewater Virginia Beach

It will be interesting to see how Tidewater Community College and the Virginia Beach Public Library fare. They are under construction and slated to open in the first half of 2013, and they have the budget for books, staff, and furniture. This project has all the earmarks of a success, but bad economic times can reshape the best of intentions.

WILL THE LIBRARY OF THE FUTURE HAVE CHAIRS AND BOOKS AND COMPUTERS AND CLASSIFICATION?

Looking farther into the future, joint libraries might not be as popular a fit because as Nancy Davenport (2006, 12) puts it: "Digital technology is redrawing the library blueprint." Because of the wide acceptance of e-content, the stacks will shrink in size and be replaced by areas that support groups of users who will need immediate (electronic) access to information. According to Davenport, the space will need to be shared with a variety of partners, and it is likely that the distinction between the library and other informal campus space will blur (2006, 13). Supersized joint libraries will no longer be in vogue due to the rapid transformation of the purpose of a library from a book distributor and storage facility to a multifunctional gathering place.

The Virtual Library

The future is arriving faster than expected. Newport Beach Public Library considered closing one of its branches and replacing it with a community center that would offer a Netflix-style electronic book ordering. City Manager Dave Kiff quips, "Shouldn't the modern library reflect what people are doing now, instead of reflecting what we might have done 20 or 30 years ago?" (Reicher 2011). However, this digital plan never materialized. Wayne State University assumed responsibility in 2009 for the Macomb County Library, but gave away the circulating books and turned it into a research and reference center with a small reference collection and a room full of computers.

The past savings that joint libraries experienced by eliminating duplicate purchases of expensive reference sets and other nonfiction materials will not be applicable to the heavily digitized libraries of the future. As the stacks shrink, so will the number, responsibilities, and work spaces needed by the staff. Renewed focus on patron convenience will force many libraries to investigate home delivery in order to match the standard of customer service that Google, Netflix, and Amazon now provide. There will no longer be separate stacks in joint libraries of Dewey and Library of Congress classified materials because both will be irrelevant to users. Arrangement of materials in libraries will be fluid and encourage browsing. Catalog systems will be replaced by more efficient big-box-store inventory methods and enhanced RFID capabilities. Instead of searching for a call number, future library systems' locations codes will inform you: "the title you want is on aisle 3, shelf 3C."

Are Partnerships Part of Our Future?

As we have said, the joint libraries are changing the way they operate. There is a trend evolving where instead of actually creating a partnership or marriage of equals, one entity will contract with another for services. University Branch, a joint library with the University of Houston-Sugar Land, Wharton County Junior College, and Fort Bend County Libraries, has the public library running the facility with the colleges contributing money for use of the library. In tough economic times, whoever can deliver services the best and cheapest will be the leader and will remain standing. The Tidewater Virginia Beach project has the college in charge, since the college contributes the lion's share of the cost of the new library. If joint libraries go into a project with their eyes wide open about who runs the library, less conflict will ensue. When North Lake Community Library was created, in fact the public library ran the facility. If the college staff knew in advance that the library would in essence be a public library, they may not have even attempted to create the joint venture.

TRUE PARTNERSHIPS ARE NOT FOR THE FAINT OF HEART

Past joint academic/public library projects have been glamorous, well-funded, and, for the most part, well liked once they opened. They have brought exciting architecture, beautiful designs, the newest technology, and a welcoming place to campuses and communities. Their attractiveness has made them hard to resist even by their staunchest critics. They have broken down the myths that they could only work in rural communities or with the smallest of libraries. The partnerships have transformed the perceptions of their employees, management, and users on what a library can be and who can best serve their informational needs. Administrators have been praised for leveraging taxpayer funds and eliminating unnecessary competition and duplication while making their libraries accessible to a greater number of users and offering a much wider range of materials and programs. They have proven to the library profession that distinctions between different types of libraries are not insurmountable.

Not for Everyone

Despite their extensive benefits, joint libraries are not suitable for every community. Many regret their loss of flexibility, find the multiple layers of decision making cumbersome and their future plans impeded. Those in charge of joint libraries will admit that managing the constant conflict is exhausting, which is one of the reasons it is hard to find experienced managers to fill the director's position in a joint library. Most institutions entering into joint agreements underestimate the adjustment time and ongoing diplomacy required when strangers are ordered to permanently live together under one roof. Some joint libraries suffer from split personalities—on the outside they look like great collaborative efforts, while on the inside they are in resistance mode and coordinate only on a minimal level. Created in more optimistic times, the annual operating costs and grandeur of joint libraries have become a major concern as libraries of all types have weathered serious and repeated cuts to their budgets.

Future joint libraries will focus on controlling costs rather than expansion of services, facilities, and goodwill. Those entering into new agreements (or up for renewal) will face intense scrutiny and require much more proof of the expected cost savings beforehand. Already joint libraries have emerged with multiple instead of single partners as costs are spread among as many participants as possible. Larger partnerships will mean more negotiations and compromises and less control and brand identity for each of the partners. Joint libraries will also become entrepreneurial opportunities for major libraries to subsidize their costs by offering service contracts rather than partnerships to nearby institutions for library services.

Then there are the digital library models that eschew books and bricks in favor of audio and e-books. Community interaction will be online as social media, rather than face-to-face in a building, whether a library building or a YMCA. Google will have scanned most books, especially the orphan books no one can locate anymore. Google will be our partner in cyberspace. Here is Google's vision from former CEO Eric Schmidt:

> Imagine sitting at your computer and, in less than a second, searching the full text of every book ever written. Imagine an historian being able to instantly find every book that mentions the Battle of Algiers. Imagine a high school student in Bangladesh discovering an out-of-print author held only in a library in Ann Arbor. Imagine one giant electronic card catalog that makes all the world's books discoverable with just a few keystrokes by anyone, anywhere, anytime. (Schmidt 2005, A18)

Although copyright vigilantes have challenged this vision in court, this is the inevitable trend called progress. The virtual library may be around the corner.

Another View

On the other hand, one can still believe in the vision and viability of joint libraries. In fact, the changes in libraries may lead to more joint ventures. Libraries serve an important need in the lives of people, particularly people who have less access to information resources. Librarians will still serve as critical guides to assisting people with information needs. People will still want face-to-face interaction. People who do not have the resources to access a computer every day will want assistance for online tasks that they are unfamiliar with. Young people who theoretically have grown up with computers still come into the libraries every day now with uncertainty in using online materials. Thus the argument cannot be made that it is only older people who haven't had exposure to technology that need the assistance of librarians and that as they die off, there will not be a need for the personal touch of librarians. The rush to assume that online resources will eliminate the need for in-person assistance sounds like the old argument from the 1970s that students could watch instructors lecture through television and that would reduce the need for teachers, which obviously never happened.

Even if the amount of space needed for physical collections is reduced, this factor may serve as a greater catalyst for joint ventures, since it might be worthwhile for a smaller library to team up with another entity. Rather than open a small library, it may make financial sense to share space. In terms of space, some libraries may decide to partner up with another library in an attempt to better utilize existing spaces.

Additionally, although a library may be purchasing electronic format items which do not take up physical space, those items still cost money. New titles are not going to be available on Google, since authors still want to get paid for their efforts. There would still be a financial incentive to share collections. It may even be cheaper to get online resources for one larger library than for two smaller libraries.

Joint libraries may be driven by a pragmatic need. The LSC-CyFair library exists, in part, because the director of the public library system realized that this was the best way to get a new library in that area of town. The University Branch of Fort Bend didn't have the land available for a new library. These are examples of the needs that drive joint libraries and that will continue to arise in the future. The commissioner for Fort Bend County related the story of getting all the librarians involved in the same room and then telling them to uncross their arms. Due to the changing landscape, librarians are going to have to uncross their arms or be swept aside. It may very well be a matter of having a small joint pie or no pie at all. Librarians who are adapting to technological changes may also adapt to changes in the "way we've always done things."

Pamela Anderson-Brulé and Brad Cox of Anderson Brulé Architects would argue that joint ventures are more likely to occur in the future because each side of a partnership gets more than they would have had alone. The interaction between the two (or more) entities encourages greater creativity. Once librarians are encouraged to think out of the box they will develop more dynamic projects, as the many examples listed in this book attest. The incentive to be more creative is only increased when budgets decrease and there is the need to do more with less. For the same reason, there is more incentive to cooperate, since the merging entities will get more for their money. The changing landscape of librarianship should lead to more reasons not to have business as usual.

Political pressures may drive partnerships as well. Politicians, particularly in today's climate, want to be seen as saving taxpayer money. Joint projects may be more likely to be funded simply because they are joint projects. The Tidewater Virginia Beach library rose to the top of the funding queue because it was a joint project.

Similarly, a joint library may be more likely to weather budget storms because it draws funding from two sources that may not be experiencing the same level of funding crisis at the same time. The joint libraries we have studied all get funding from two different entities. In the case of the Lone Star system, although they have suffered from the same decreases in property tax revenue that plague Harris County, property taxes are a smaller percentage of the college system's revenues.

The advanced strategy planning that was done in San Jose and Virginia Beach allowed the libraries to work through many of the issues that would come up in the day-to-day running of the library later. Although this process still required the initial vision and commitment from upper management, having the opportunity to resolve concerns in a series of meetings before beginning to work together ameliorated the eventual pairings. If the library merger is a marriage, the proper prenuptial agreement may obviate the later divorce.

For each successive joint library that occurs, the process of developing the new library should get easier. Pamela Anderson-Brulé stated that although they did not learn specific solutions for merging two libraries from the MLK experience that carried over to the Tidewater Virginia Beach project, they did know which questions to ask in the process (Pamela Anderson-Brulé and Brad Cox, pers. comm.). By studying how other libraries have merged or developed a single joint library, a library considering this project can learn how to avoid mistakes and go through a smoother process. It is hoped that this book will assist librarians and administrators considering joint libraries to see that the joint process is not a scary impossible nightmare, but rather a possible dream.

DON QUIXOTES OF THE LIBRARY WORLD

There will always be the adventuresome, like the Tidewater Virginia Beach project, who dream big and see the future as "more than a library" (Virginia Beach 2005). There will always be the intrepid visionaries who forge ahead with their impossible dreams. Even though Lamar Veatch's and Jim Horton's vision for North Lake was a "glorious failure," it showed wonderful possibilities despite the naysayers. Lone Star-CyFair's Earl Campa believes that to not have joined with Harris County would have been a crime and a supreme disservice to its students and community (Earl Campa, pers. comm.). While joint libraries are wonderful endeavors, which may or may not be a part of our future, they also represent the best of human cooperation for the greater good. This book is dedicated to these Don Quixotes of the library world.

APPENDIX A
CY-FAIR COLLEGE AND HARRIS COUNTY AGREEMENT

 Appendixes available for download as editable Word documents at alaeditions.org/webextras/.

INTERLOCAL AGREEMENT FOR
CONSTRUCTION, USE AND MAINTENANCE OF LIBRARY FACILITIES

THE STATE OF TEXAS   §
                  §
COUNTY OF HARRIS   §

      THIS INTERLOCAL AGREEMENT FOR CONSTRUCTION, USE AND MAINTENANCE OF LIBRARY FACILITIES ("Agreement") is made and entered by and between North Harris Montgomery Community College District ("District"), operating under Article VII of the Texas Constitution and Chapter 130.004(a), Texas Education Code, and Harris County ("County"), a body corporate and politic under the laws of the State of Texas, as authorized under an Order of the Harris County Commissioners Court;

<u>W I T N E S S E T H</u>:

      WHEREAS, the District is constructing various academic and educational facilities at its campus at Cy-Fair College ("College"), an institution of higher education located at 9191 Barker Cypress Road in Harris County, for the purposes of (a) serving its local taxing district and service areas in Texas, (b) satisfying the College's accreditation requirements, which include the maintenance and operation of a college level library, and (c) serving the needs and providing the educational resources as prescribed under Chapter 130, Texas Educational Code; and

      WHEREAS, the County operates the Harris County Public Library ("HCPL"), a network of community-focused libraries, to help meet the diverse informational, educational, and recreational needs of Harris County residents; and

      WHEREAS, District has deemed it necessary and a requirement of its statutory mandate to construct a college-level library at the College campus; and

      WHEREAS, County has identified a need for a branch public library, as part of the HCPL system, in the general geographic vicinity of the College; and

      WHEREAS, the District has prepared drawings and specifications ("Drawings and Specifications") for both (i) a two-story library building consisting of approximately 107,500 square feet of space, of which approximately 78,500 square feet of space will consist of a library (the "Joint Library"), at the College, and (ii) a Parking Area containing approximately one hundred-fifty parking spaces to accommodate general public use (the Joint Library and Parking Area collectively being called "Joint Library Facility"), which Drawings and Specifications have been approved by the County, and the District has begun construction of the Joint Library Facility; and

      WHEREAS, it is to the mutual benefit of the District and County and their constituencies to plan, design, construct, furnish, equip, staff, operate and maintain the Joint Library in accordance with the terms contained herein and to have the Joint Library serve, and be available to, not only the District and its students, but all users of the HCPL; and

      WHEREAS, by Order of the Commissioners Court of the County dated January 15, 2002, the County was authorized to reimburse the District the sum of $1,000,000.00 for re-design fees, photocopying, graphics and related expenses, approximately one hundred-fifty parking spaces in the south student parking lot to accommodate general public use of the Joint Library, additional structural steel and foundation work, and furniture selection and coordination; and

164

WHEREAS, the County is willing to contribute the sum of $4,440,000.00, which includes the previously approved sum of $1,000,000.00, $3,050,000.00 toward the cost of construction of the Joint Library Facility and $390,000.00 for the purchase of fixtures and furnishings; and

WHEREAS, the County is willing to contribute $322,764.00 as the start-up cost of staffing requirements and related expenses including, but not limited to, supplies, travel, training, and janitorial, maintenance and utilities, as agreed to by the Steering Committee, for the Joint Library covering the start-up period of March 1, 2003 to August 31, 2003; and

WHEREAS, the County is willing to contribute $659,867.00 toward the cost of operating and maintaining the Joint Library for the period of September 1, 2003 to February 29, 2004;

NOW, THEREFORE, in consideration of the mutual covenants, agreements and benefits to both parties, and in order to meet and satisfy the educational mandates and critical needs and goals as set forth above, District and County intend, pursuant to this Agreement, to jointly combine their resources and efforts to design, construct, equip, staff, operate and maintain the Joint Library that will contain aspects both of the College - to provide the necessary library resources and research materials to fulfill the College's mandate under Chapter 130, Texas Educational Code and the historic and prospective missions of the College, and of the County - to provide the necessary library resources to fulfill the County's mission to help meet the diverse informational, educational, and recreational needs of the County residents with an integral unit of the HCPL system, it is agreed as follows:

I

A.   On or before the sixtieth day after the approval of this contract by the Commissioners Court of the County and by the District, the County will pay to the District the sum of $4,440,000.00 that includes: (i) $4,050,000.00 (which includes the hereinabove mentioned sum of $3,050,000.00 plus the previously approved sum of $1,000,000.00) for all "soft and hard costs" of construction of the Joint Library Facility; and (ii) $390,000.00 for the purchase of fixtures and furnishings. "Soft Costs" mean expenses incurred for design professionals including architects, engineers, surveyors, special design consultants, construction management consultants, permit and review fees, impact fees, legal and professional fees, recording fees, costs for tests performed before, during, and after construction, fees paid to moving companies, and applicable taxes, if any. "Hard Costs" mean those costs relating to fees paid to contractors for labor, materials, equipment, overhead, and profit, fees paid directly to material suppliers for materials and equipment, utilities, and applicable taxes, if any. The District will establish and place the funds in a separate interest bearing account from which such monies will be withdrawn during the construction period for the soft and hard costs of the Joint Library Facility. The District will be responsible for all soft and hard costs of constructing the Joint Library Facility in excess of $4,050,000.00. Said sum of $4,050,000.00 shall be the maximum amount contributed by the County toward the construction costs for the Joint Library Facility. If the County's contribution of $4,050,000.00, including interest earned thereon, exceeds the soft and hard costs of the Joint Library Facility, the District shall refund such excess to the County.

B.   The County shall be solely responsible for the acquisition, installation and payment of self-checkout equipment, staff and circulation computers, public access computers, audio-visual equipment, software and other related items for incorporation and placement in the Joint Library. The standards and specifications for this equipment shall be coordinated with the College.

C.   On or before the sixtieth day after the approval of this contract by the Commissioners Court of the County and by the District, the County will pay to the District for the first partial

2

year of operation of the Joint Library, March 1, 2003 to August 31, 2003, the sum of $322,764.00 as the County's part of the start-up cost of operating the Joint Library, said sum to include costs for staffing requirements, salaries, employee benefits, and reasonable and necessary employee related expenses including, but not limited to, supplies, training, travel, and the janitorial, maintenance and utilities, as agreed to by the Steering Committee (hereinafter referenced and created). As used herein, "staffing requirements" include the library administrative and clerical staffs and the Joint Library Director. If there are unexpended County funds remaining at the end of the District's fiscal year ending August 31, 2003, after the payment of all the first partial year's start-up operating expenses, the District shall refund such excess funds to the County, without demand, within forty-five (45) days after the end of the fiscal year.

D.   At such time as set by the Steering Committee, the County may, at no cost to the District, provide public library books and materials (print and electronic) for the Joint Library in a fashion equal to or better than that of a HCPL library of equal size. This option will be for the initial year of operation of the Joint Library and shall continue during the term of this Agreement, both in terms of new orders and maintenance of the currency of the public library collection.

II

The District will administer the construction of the Joint Library Facility and perform construction inspection, materials testing and surveying, if appropriate, for the Joint Library Facility. The District will construct the Joint Library Facility in accordance with the Drawings and Specifications. The District may make minor changes in the drawings and specifications, which it deems necessary or desirable during the construction of the Joint Library Facility, so long as the changes do not materially affect the scope of the work, and the District notifies the County of such changes.

III

The District will cause its Cy-Fair College President, or said President's designee, and the County will cause its HCPL Library Director, or said Director's designee, to serve on a Joint Steering Committee ("Steering Committee"), whose purpose or function is as follows:

A.   Hold regular meetings, with a minimum of one meeting every three months, to discuss the mutual needs and goals of the District and the County as they relate to the Joint Library Facility;

B.   Foster and develop a unique, integrated library system;

C.   Develop and propose annual Joint Library budgets;

D.   Establish the days and hours of operation for the Joint Library;

E.   Adopt Joint Library lending procedures appropriate to the operation of the Joint Library, and integrate the book (print and electronic) lending procedures and practices of the District and County in such a manner as to apply uniformly to the general public, students and faculty;

F.   Attempt to resolve (i) conflicts that may arise under this Agreement, and (ii) inconsistencies between the polices of District and County as to book and material loans, returns and renewals, and access to Joint Library materials, computers, the internet and other services, for members of the general public and the College community;

G.   Determine what furniture, furnishings, fixtures, computer equipment, library supplies, book collections (print and electronic) and library materials (and replacements and repairs thereto) are needed for the Joint Library, and recommend which party shall purchase same;

3

H.   Develop, review and revise as necessary, procedures and policies regarding the purchasing of the various library books (print and electronic) and materials deemed necessary or desirable for the Joint Library; and

I.   Assure that staff of the Joint Library are trained in the policies and procedures of the Joint Library and that the staff attends appropriate meetings and training sessions that the Steering Committee may require.

The District and the County may designate other members of the Steering Committee, upon notice to the other party. The members of the Steering Committee may designate other persons to assist them. Neither the Steering Committee nor the members thereof are authorized to contractually bind either the District or the County. In the event the members of the Steering Committee are unable to reach a consensus, the Cy-Fair College President and the HCPL Library Director will attempt to resolve the conflict.

IV

On or about June 1, 2003, the District will submit to the County a statement in the amount of $659,867.00 for the County's contribution toward the operation and maintenance of the Joint Library, for the period commencing September 1, 2003 and ending February 29, 2004. Within thirty (30) days after the receipt of the statement, the County will pay said statement, subject to Paragraphs VII and VIII below.

V

(a)   On or about October 1 of each year during which this Agreement remains in effect, starting with October 1, 2003, the Steering Committee will estimate the projected costs of (i) janitorial, maintenance and utilities for the Joint Library during the next fiscal year of the District (September 1 through August 31), and (ii) staffing and all other costs of operating the Joint Library during said fiscal year, allocating such costs between the parties, and will notify the District and County of such amounts, and the amount of the allocation to the County. Such costs under item (ii) include technology, furnishings, supplies and books and materials (print and electronic), and any other general operating costs, but excludes projected repairs and modifications pursuant to Paragraph X. On or before March 15 of each of the succeeding years that the Agreement remains in effect, the County will have the option of issuing a purchase order in the amount of the County's share, and obtaining the County Auditor's certification of such funds, subject to Paragraphs VII and VIII, in an amount equal to 35% of such estimated amount for janitorial, maintenance and utilities, and that portion of the staffing and other expenses allocated to the County by the Steering Committee. For each of the District's fiscal years while this Agreement is in effect and in which the County exercises its option of issuing a purchase order pursuant to this subparagraph, the County will pay the amounts allocated in four quarterly installments within thirty days following receipt of each quarterly statement from the District.

(b)   For example, on or about October 1, 2003, the Steering Committee will estimate the projected costs of (i) janitorial, maintenance and utilities for the Joint Library during the upcoming fiscal year of the District (September 1, 2004 through August 31, 2005), and (ii) staffing and all other costs of operating the Joint Library, excluding projected repairs and modifications pursuant to Paragraph X, during the said fiscal year, allocating such costs between the District and the County, and will notify the District and the County of said amounts and the amount of the allocation to the County. On or about March 15, 2004, the County will have the option of issuing a purchase order in the amount of the County's share, and obtaining the County Auditor's certification of such funds, subject to Paragraphs VII and VIII below, in an amount equal to 35% of such estimated amount for janitorial, maintenance and utilities, and that portion of the staffing and other expenses allocated to the County by the Steering Committee. On or about April 1, 2004, July 1, 2004, October 1, 2004 and January 1, 2005, the District will submit

4

to the County a statement for ¼ of said amount. If the County exercises its option pursuant to this subparagraph, the County will pay each of said installments within thirty (30) days after the receipt of the statement for said installment amount.

(c)   Beginning in 2004 and continuing each year thereafter while this Agreement remains in effect, the same procedure as set out in subparagraph (b) above will be followed by the parties for purposes of determining the amount of the County's contribution to the Joint Library and method of paying thereof. Thus, prior to each October 1 while this Agreement remains in effect, the Steering Committee will send notices to the County and District regarding projected costs of operating and maintaining the Joint Library during the next fiscal year of the District. The County may exercise its options on or about March 15 of each of the following calendar years while this Agreement is in effect, the District will issue statements, and the County will make payments for each of the fiscal years for which it exercises its options, in a manner similar to the manner set out in subparagraph (b) above.

VI

So long as the County exercises the options to contribute funds to the District for the operation and maintenance of the Joint Library pursuant to this Agreement, the District must continue to operate the Joint Library Facility in accordance with this Agreement.

VII

The sums paid by the County to the District pursuant to the above paragraphs shall have subtracted from them the cost to the County of cataloging and processing the College's materials collection.

VIII

The District will expend funds paid to it by the County under Paragraphs IV and V only for operating and maintaining the Joint Library Facility. The District is not authorized to expend any funds paid to it by the County under Paragraphs IV and V for any expense or cost of operating the Joint Library unless the District pays the expense or cost of (i) janitorial, maintenance and utilities using 65% District funds and 35% County funds, and (ii) staffing and all other costs of operating the Joint Library in accordance with the Steering Committee's allocation between the County and District. If any funds provided under Paragraphs IV and V remain unexpended at the end of any year for which they are provided, the District will, at the option of the County, either return such unexpended funds to the County, or credit such unexpended funds against the payments to be made by the County to the District pursuant to Paragraph V. At such time as the County fails to exercise any of its options to pay the District the funds as provided for under Paragraphs IV or V, the sole and exclusive remedy of the District is to terminate this Agreement by providing thirty days advance notice of termination to the County. In the event of such termination of this Agreement and the termination of the operation of a Joint Library hereunder, unless the County requests otherwise in writing to the District, the District will allow the Joint Library to be available for use by the public for a period of three (3) years from the date the notice of termination is given by the County. Provided however, incident to such use by the public, the District shall not be obligated to acquire or purchase any particular books (print and electronic) or periodicals, supplies and/or materials for the public's use. Further, such use of the Joint Library by the public in such event will be subject to and in accordance with the District's policies, rules, regulations and hours of operation, which shall be applied in a non-discriminatory fashion as to the public. Further, it is not the intention of the parties, and the District and County do disclaim any rights or privileges hereunder that may be granted unto or in favor of any person or entity, other than the parties to this Agreement.

5

IX

The County and its representatives have the right to review and audit all books, records, vouchers and documents of whatever nature related to the District's performance under this Agreement, during the period of performance of the Agreement and for three years thereafter, or for so long as there exists any dispute or litigation arising from this Agreement.

X

In the event a capital repair, defined as a repair costing in excess of $1,000.00 and caused by ordinary wear and tear and not necessitated by the District's failure to properly operate and maintain the Joint Library Facility or otherwise due to the fault of the District or its employees, to the Joint Library Facility is required during the term of this Agreement, the following provisions shall apply:

a) District shall manage a program of capital repairs for the Joint Library Facility during the term of this Agreement. During the term of this Agreement, 65% of the cost of the capital repairs will be allocated to the District and 35% of the cost of such capital repairs will be allocated to the County, subject to the hereinbelow provided conditions. In the event, however, District adds onto or expands the building containing the Joint Library, without increasing the size of the Joint Library itself, such percentages and allocation amounts will be re-computed based on the expanded size of the said building. The cost of all capital and other repairs for any given year are those costs that are necessary to keep the Library Facility open and operational for the students, faculty, guests and visitors of the College and the general public and users of the HCPL branch.

In the event repairs to the Joint Library Facility are required due to the District's failure to properly maintain the Joint Library Facility or are otherwise due to the fault of the District or its employees, the District shall manage and perform such repairs. The County shall have no responsibility to pay for costs of such repairs.

(b)   If District determines that the Joint Library Facility is in need of capital repairs, it will prepare a list of such proposed capital repairs (together with an estimated cost thereof), and submit a copy of same to the County. The list shall specify the priority for each proposed capital repair. The County may propose modifications to the list and other capital repairs that District may not have included on the list.

Following the County's review of the list of recommended proposed capital repairs and the submission of any proposed capital repairs of its own, District and the County shall, in good faith, attempt to agree on those capital repairs that will be necessary to keep the Joint Library Facility open and operational together with the estimated cost(s) thereof.

(c)   If, within one hundred-eighty days after County's receipt of the list under Paragraph X(b) above, the County and the District are unable to enter into either an amendment to this Agreement or a separate agreement in regard to the determination of necessary capital repairs, the District may notify the County that it intends to perform the capital repairs itself. The District shall have the right to perform such capital repairs, at its sole cost and expense, after giving the County at least 30 days notice of its intention to do so. If the District and the County do not enter into an amendment to this agreement or a separate agreement under which the County agrees to pay a portion of such costs within ninety (90) days after such notification, the District's sole and exclusive remedy shall be the same as that provided in Paragraph VIII above.

6

XI

The Joint Library will be named and known as the "Harris County Public Library – Cy-Fair College Branch." In the event of termination of this Agreement or in the event of default by the County or the County's decision not to appropriate funds for the Joint Library at any time in the future, the Joint Library name "Harris County Public Library – Cy-Fair College Branch" will be removed from the Joint Library Facility and the Land, in the discretion of the District, subject to the time period set forth in Article VIII.

XII

During and after construction of the Joint Library, and during the term of this Agreement, the District and County may each display a plaque at the Joint Library indicating that District and County have expended funds for the construction of the Joint Library, and that the Joint Library is available to the general public.

XIII

There shall be two signs at the driveway and building entrances of the Joint Library, one signifying the name "Learning Commons" and another signifying the name "Harris County Public Library Branch," or a specific branch name as designated by the County. The size, style, placement, material and format of the signs will be consistent with the signage at the College and subject to the review and reasonable approval of the College President.

XIV

At all times during the term of this Agreement, the shared goals of the District and County shall be to (a) strive to meet the Joint Library support needs of the College and its students, faculty and guests, and of Harris County and the residents of the County; and (b) share certain costs, library collections and materials, library facilities, staffing and purchasing, with a minimizing of duplication of services and functions as much as possible.

XV

(a) When the District purchases materials for the collection, it will catalog the materials, or have one or more of the vendors it selects catalog the materials, using the Dewey Decimal System in a manner, except as approved by the Steering Committee, that matches the County's materials collection. The County will catalog the materials purchased by the District for ongoing maintenance of the District's collections. Wherever possible, the District will arrange for its vendors to handle materials processing, labeling, jacketing, stamping and security targets and bars in accordance with the County's guidelines. If a vendor of the District declines or is unable to perform such tasks, then and in that event, the District may ask the County to perform such tasks.

(b) The County will catalog and process the materials it orders and will arrange to have those materials delivered to the County Library Administrative Office.

(c) Neither the District nor the County is responsible for the payment of the other party's purchases except as may be provided elsewhere in this Agreement.

XVI

During the term of this Agreement, the District has the exclusive control and supervision of the Joint Library, except as otherwise provided herein. The District shall at all times be solely

7

responsible for the security of the Joint Library Facility. The District, with the advice from HCPL, shall adopt a security plan prior to the opening of the Joint Library to the general public.

XVII

The Joint Library employees shall be employees of the District. The District shall require the Joint Library employees to work together, regardless of their particular responsibilities. The District shall take steps to ensure that the Joint Library Director has public library experience. The Joint Library employees shall be subject, in a non-discriminatory fashion, to all rules, regulations, terms of employment, salary, benefits, supervision, discipline, discharge, personal and reference investigations and other terms of employment, as established from time to time by District. Salary and benefits of all Joint Library employees shall be in accordance with the compensation and benefits plans adopted by District from time to time.

XVIII

The District shall own and hold sole title to the land upon which the building housing the Joint Library Facility is constructed, together with the building itself and all improvements to the land upon which the Joint Library Facility is constructed.

XIX

In performing their obligations hereunder, the District and County will comply with all applicable Federal, State, County and City ordinances, rules and regulations.

XX

It is the intent of the District and the County to provide unfettered access to all Joint Library materials and services (computer and internet, for example) for all members of the general public and the College community, according to their library card profile. However, access to adult-oriented materials and websites by minors shall be subject to controls in accordance with District and HCPL's policies. The computers located in the children's room will be filtered.

XXI

The Joint Library will be open to the use of the general public. No person who is eligible to use the County public library shall be required to pay a fee to the District to use the Joint Library. However, the Joint Library, through the Steering Committee and/or the Joint Library Director, may charge certain fees for printing, copying and similar consumable supplies.

XXII

The parties, subject to their budgeting process and funding, intend to operate the Joint Library in accordance with the following guidelines, which guidelines shall be periodically reviewed and may be altered or deleted by the Joint Steering Committee, except in the event of creation of financial obligation on either the District or the County, without necessitating a formal amendment to this Agreement:

A. The County will furnish and maintain a dedicated T-1 line for computer connection to the Horizon system, along with a firewall to restrict access to the County's computer network.
B. The County will furnish and maintain the computer hardware that is connected to the Horizon system.
C. The District will maintain the public access computers.

8

D. The District will develop procedures whereby patrons and students may reserve open computers for a specific period of time.
E. The District will develop a printing/debit card system for copying and computer printing.
F. The District will provide each public access computer with two icons, one for the County collection and the other for the District's college library collection.
G. The District will place instructions at each public access computer for patron and student use.
H. The District will activate its Resource Sharing System in order to allow students and patrons to loan items between the College and other District college libraries.
I. The County and the District will continue their current courier routes. The County and the District will include both the District's main administrative office and the College Campus in their courier service routes.
J. The District will keep and maintain in good repair the exterior walls, exterior doors, exterior doorways, elevators, windows, roof, structural portions, heating equipment, air conditioning equipment, plumbing, lobby, wiring and electrical equipment, interior walls, ceilings, floors, interior doors, interior doorways, hallways, restrooms, carpets, floor coverings and all other parts of said library building.
K. The District will keep and maintain in good repair, the driveways, walkways and entrances on the tract or parcel of land on which the Joint Library is situated, and also keep the same neat and clean.
L. The District will keep and maintain in good repair and condition the lighting fixtures in the Joint Library, including, but not limited to furnishing and installing light producing elements.
M. The District will operate the air conditioning and heating equipment so as to maintain the air temperature in the Joint Library between 65 to 75 degrees Fahrenheit during regular library hours. However, in the event any state, federal or municipal law, rule or regulation applicable to the Joint Library required the maintenance of the air temperature therein within a range other than that hereinabove specified, then the air temperature range will be maintained as near to the temperature range set forth above as may be permitted under such law, rule or regulation.
N. The District will comply with all requirements of the Americans With Disabilities Act, the Texas Architectural Barriers Act, and all other valid laws, ordinances, regulations and other requirements, now or hereafter in force, of all federal, state and local governmental bodies and agencies which are application to the Joint Library, including, but not limited to, the lobby, halls, stairways, elevators, restrooms, driveways, walkways and entrances on the tract of land on which the Joint Library is situated. District is wholly responsible for performing all alterations that need to be made to the Joint Library and areas described above, to accommodate the members of the public using the Joint Library. The cost of performing the alterations will be allocated between the parties by the Steering Committee in the same manner as capital repairs are allocated. No provision in this Agreement will be construed in any manner as permitting, consenting to or authorizing District to violate requirements under either such Act, and any provision in the Agreement which could arguably be construed as authorizing a violation of either Act will be interpreted in a manner which permits compliance with such Act and is hereby amended to permit such compliance.
O. The District shall issue library cards for the users of the Joint Library, being the students and faculty of the College, and the general public. The District shall issue the cards in accordance with the respective policies of District and the HCPL system. The District will merge the computerization of the Joint Library card issuance, validation and usage for the borrowers of the Joint Library into the HCPL computers and records.
P. The District shall adopt and enforce a schedule of fines and penalties regarding overdue, lost or damaged books and other library materials (print and electronic) consistent with the schedule adopted by HCPL, from time to time, for its branch library system. Revenue collected by the District for fines and penalties will be used for the operation, maintenance and repair of the Joint Library.
Q. The District will provide janitorial services for the Joint Library in accordance with the College's custodial standards.

9

XXIII

The District will, at its own expense, maintain a liability insurance policy covering the Joint Library with coverage in the amount of not less than $200,000 for injuries to or death of any one person, not less than $600,000 for injuries to or death of more than one person and not less than $200,000 for any injury to or destruction of property in any one accident or occurrence, or in the amounts of twice the amount of the County's maximum limitations of liability under Section 101.001 et seq., Texas Civil Practice and Remedies Code Annotated, as amended, whichever is greater. Said policy will name the County as an additional insured. Within thirty (30) days after the commencement of the term of this Agreement, the District will furnish a photocopy of the certificate of the insurance to the Director of the HCPL.

XXIV

Neither the District nor the County shall use or store or cause to be created any Hazardous Substances in, on or near the Joint Library Facility, with the sole exception of reasonably necessary substances that are kept in reasonably necessary quantities for normal library operations, provided that their use and storage are in accordance with all applicable laws. "Hazardous Substances" means any hazardous substances, sewage, petroleum products, hazardous materials, toxic substances or any pollutants or substances defined as hazardous or toxic in accordance with federal or state laws and regulations.

XXV

It is not the intention of the District and County (or any instrumentalities or agencies thereof) to create a partnership or association. The duties and liabilities of the parties hereto are intended to be separate and not joint or collective. Nothing contained in this Agreement or in any document made pursuant hereto shall ever be construed to create a partnership or association or impose a partnership duty, obligation or liability with respect to any one or more of the parties hereto.

XXVI

(A)   Should the Joint Library be destroyed or damaged, or the right of ingress and egress be impaired, so that the Joint Library is rendered unfit for use by County, or should any governmental body, agency, department, or official determine the Joint Library to be a fire hazard, or for any other reason whatsoever to be unsuitable for the use or uses for which the County contemplates using same, then and in any such event, the County will have no further duty to pay additional sums of money to the District during the period of destruction or damaged condition, impairment, or unsuitability. Likewise, the District shall be relieved from any duties or obligations placed upon it under this Agreement during such period. Further, in such event as set forth in this paragraph, this Agreement may be terminated at the option of County, and the District will return to the County the unexpended funds paid by the County to the District pursuant to this Agreement. The County's exercise of any of the rights or options under this paragraph will not in any way prejudice the County's right to recover damages which the County has sustained as a result of District's refusal or failure to perform, and the rights and options under this paragraph are cumulative with, and not in lieu of, other remedies provided by law.

(B)   The District agrees to maintain fire and extended insurance coverage on the Joint Library in the same fashion as it maintains insurance for its other facilities, either under a blanket insurance policy or separate and distinct insurance policy. In the event the Joint Library is destroyed or substantially damaged as set forth in this article and the District elects not to re-build or repair the Joint Library, then in that event the County will be entitled to, and the District

10

will pay the County without demand, a sum equal to $4,440,000.00 or 35% of any insurance proceeds collected or received by the District, whichever is less.

XXVII

In the event of termination of this Agreement for any reason, the County may remove all personal property that the County owns or had placed in the Joint Library, and the County may remove any "Harris County Public Library Branch" or similar signage in the driveway and building entrances of the Joint Library, even though any of such items may be attached to the land.

XXVIII

All notices and communications under this Agreement will be mailed by certified mail, return receipt requested, or delivered to the County at the following address:

Harris County Commissioners Court
Harris County Administration Building
1001 Preston Avenue, 9th Floor
Houston, Texas 77002
Attention: Clerk of Commissioners Court

All notices and communications under this Agreement will be mailed by certified mail, return receipt requested, or delivered to the District at the following address:

North Harris Montgomery Community College District
250 N. Sam Houston Parkway East
Houston, Texas 77060
Attention: President, Cy-Fair College

Notice will be considered given and completed upon deposit of the notice in a United States Postal Service receptacle.

XXIX

The District has budgeted or shall budget the sums necessary to pay its obligations under its current fiscal year.

XXX

The County represents that it has current funds available in the sum of $5,422,631.00 to meet its obligations under this Agreement, plus such additional sums that may from time to time be appropriated by the Commissioners Court in its sole option. Although the County may expend additional funds, it is understood that notwithstanding any other provision of this Agreement, the County is not obligated by this Agreement to expend funds in excess of the said budgeted sum.

XXXI

No party hereto shall make, in whole or in part, any assignment of this Agreement or any obligation hereunder without the prior written consent of the other party hereto.

11

XXXII

This instrument contains the entire agreement between the parties relating to the rights herein granted and the obligations herein assumed. Any modifications concerning this instrument are of no force and effect excepting a subsequent modification in writing, signed by both parties hereto.

IN TESTIMONY OF WHICH, this Agreement has been executed in duplicate counterparts, each to have the force and effect of an original as follows:

(a)   It has been executed on behalf of the County on the _____ day of   FEB 1 8 2003 , 2003, by the County Judge of Harris County, Texas, pursuant to an Order of the Commissioners Court of Harris County, Texas, authorizing such execution; and

(b)   It has been executed on behalf of the District on the _____ day of ___FEB 0 6 2003__, 2003, by its _____, and attested by its _____, pursuant to an order of the Board of Trustees of the District authorizing such execution.

APPROVED AS TO FORM:

MIKE STAFFORD
County Attorney

By _____
WILLIAM R. BRUYERE
Real Property Section Chief
I/NHMCCD8   02RPD0006   02/06/03

HARRIS COUNTY

By _____
ROBERT ECKELS, County Judge

ATTEST:

_____

By _____
LARRY SHRYOCK, CHAIR

APPROVED:

_____
CATHERINE S. PARK, Director
Harris County Public Library

APPROVED:

_____
DIANE K. TROYER, President
Cy-Fair College

AUDITOR'S CERTIFICATE

I certify that funds are available to pay Harris County's obligation of $5,422,631.00 hereunder.

_____
TOMMY TOMPKINS, County Auditor

12

175

THE STATE OF TEXAS §

COUNTY OF HARRIS §

APPROVE _____

Recorded Vol. _____ Page _____

The Commissioners Court of Harris County, Texas, convened at a meeting of said Court at the Harris County Administration Building in the City of Houston, Texas, on the ____ day of ___ FEB 18 2003 ___, 2003, with the following members present, to-wit:

Robert Eckels	County Judge
El Franco Lee	Commissioner, Precinct No. 1
Sylvia Garcia	Commissioner, Precinct No. 2
Steve Radack	Commissioner, Precinct No. 3
Jerry Eversole	Commissioner, Precinct No. 4

and the following members absent, to-wit: *None* _____, constituting a quorum, when among other business, the following was transacted:

ORDER AUTHORIZING THE COUNTY JUDGE TO EXECUTE AN AGREEMENT BY AND BETWEEN HARRIS COUNTY AND NORTH HARRIS MONTGOMERY COMMUNITY COLLEGE DISTRICT

Commissioner *Radack* introduced an order and made a motion that the same be adopted. Commissioner *Lee* seconded the motion for adoption of the order. The motion, carrying with it the adoption of the order, prevailed by the following vote:

	Yes	No	Abstain
Judge Eckels	☑	☐	☐
Comm. Lee	☑	☐	☐
Comm. Garcia	☑	☐	☐
Comm. Radack	☑	☐	☐
Comm. Eversole	☑	☐	☐

The County Judge thereupon announced that the motion had duly and lawfully carried and that the order had been duly and lawfully adopted. The order thus adopted follows:

WHEREAS, the District is constructing various academic and educational facilities at its campus at Cy-Fair College ("College"), an institution of higher education located at 9191 Barker Cypress Road in Harris County, for the purposes of (a) serving its local taxing district and service areas in Texas; (b) satisfying the College's accreditation requirements, which include the maintenance and operation of a college level library, and (c) serving the needs and providing the educational resources as prescribed under Chapter 130, Texas Educational Code; and

WHEREAS, the County operates the Harris County Public Library ("HCPL"), a network of community-focused libraries, to help meet the diverse informational, educational, and recreational needs of Harris County residents; and

WHEREAS, District has deemed it necessary and a requirement of its statutory mandate to construct a college-level library at the College campus; and

WHEREAS, County has identified a need for a branch public library, as part of the HCPL system, in the general geographic vicinity of the College; and

WHEREAS, the District has prepared drawings and specifications ("Drawings and Specifications") for both (i) a two-story library building consisting of approximately 107,500 square feet of space, of which approximately 78,500 square feet of space will consist of a library (the "Joint Library"), at the College, and (ii) a Parking Area containing approximately one hundred-fifty parking spaces to accommodate general public use (the Joint Library and Parking Area collectively being called "Joint Library Facility"), which Drawings and Specifications have been approved by the County, and the District has begun construction of the Joint Library Facility; and

WHEREAS, it is to the mutual benefit of the District and County and their constituencies to plan, design, construct, furnish, equip, staff, operate and maintain the Joint Library in accordance with the terms contained herein and to have the Joint Library serve, and be available to, not only the District and its students, but all users of the HCPL; and

WHEREAS, by Order of the Commissioners Court of the County dated January 15, 2002, the County was authorized to reimburse the District the sum of $1,000,000.00 for re-design fees, photocopying, graphics and related expenses, approximately one hundred-fifty parking spaces in the south student parking lot to accommodate general public use of the Joint Library, additional structural steel and foundation work, and furniture selection and coordination; and

WHEREAS, the County is willing to contribute the sum of $4,440,000.00, which includes the previously approved sum of $1,000,000.00, $3,050,000.00 toward the cost of construction of the Joint Library Facility and $390,000.00 for the purchase of fixtures and furnishings; and

WHEREAS, the County is willing to contribute $322,764.00 as the start-up cost of staffing requirements and related expenses including, but not limited to, supplies, travel, training, and janitorial, maintenance and utilities, as agreed to by the Steering Committee, for the Joint Library covering the start-up period of March 1, 2003 to August 31, 2003; and

WHEREAS, the County is willing to contribute $659,867.00 toward the cost of operating and maintaining the Joint Library for the period of September 1, 2003 to February 29, 2004;

NOW, THEREFORE, BE IT ORDERED BY THE COMMISSIONERS COURT OF HARRIS COUNTY, TEXAS THAT:

Section 1:   The recitals set forth in this Order are true and correct.

Section 2:   The Harris County Judge is hereby authorized to execute, for and on behalf of Harris County, an Agreement by and between Harris County and North Harris Montgomery Community College District, said Agreement being incorporated herein by reference and made a part hereof for all intents and purposes as though fully set forth herein word for word.

APPENDIX B
CITY OF IRVING AND NORTH LAKE COLLEGE AGREEMENT

 Appendixes available for download as editable Word documents at alaeditions.org/webextras/.

CITY OF IRVING

COUNCIL RESOLUTION NO. 6-18-98- 317

BE IT RESOLVED BY THE CITY COUNCIL OF THE CITY OF IRVING, TEXAS:

SECTION I.   THAT the City Council hereby approves the attached Intergovernmental Agreement between the City of Irving and the Dallas County Community College District for the development, maintenance, operation and use of a Community Library on the North Lake College campus and the Mayor is authorized to execute said agreement.

SECTION II.   THAT this resolution shall take effect from and after its final date of passage, and it is accordingly so ordered.

PASSED AND APPROVED BY THE CITY COUNCIL OF THE CITY OF IRVING, TEXAS, this 18th day of June, A.D., 1998.

MORRIS H. PARRISH
MAYOR

ATTEST:

Janice Carroll, CMC
City Secretary

APPROVED AS TO FORM:

Don J. Rorschach
City Attorney

179

North Lake Community Library
Intergovernmental Agreement

THIS AGREEMENT, is made and entered into this 18th day of June, 1998, by and between the DALLAS COMMUNITY COLLEGE DISTRICT in behalf of its NORTH LAKE COLLEGE, a Texas political subdivision of higher education, 5001 N. MacArthur, Irving, Texas (hereinafter referred to as "College"), and the CITY OF IRVING, TEXAS, a municipal corporation in behalf of the IRVING PUBLIC LIBRARY (hereinafter referred to as "City")

WHEREAS, College and City desire to: (1) plan a site on College's campus in Irving, Texas for a Community Library; (2) design and construct a Community Library of a size to be determined; (3) furnish and equip the Community Library by incorporating the College Library's existing furnishings and purchase additional, new furnishings; (4) incorporate the College Library's existing materials and purchase additional, new materials; and (5) staff, operate and maintain the Community Library for the benefit of general public of the City and the students, faculty and staff of the College; and

WHEREAS, the College and City desire to enter into this Agreement in order to set forth their respective rights and obligations concerning the development, maintenance, operation and use of the Community Library; and

WHEREAS, the land upon which the Community Library will be built is owned by the College; and

WHEREAS, the Community Library building will be owned by the College, and

WHEREAS, the parties are authorized to enter into intergovernmental agreements to provide any function, service or facility; and

WHEREAS, the College is required to have a library as part of its accreditation as an institution of higher education under the Southern Association of Colleges and Schools; and

WHEREAS, the College anticipates that this Community Library will serve that purpose; and

WHEREAS, the City has experienced significant population growth and desires to provide more convenient and improved library services to all citizens of Irving; and

WHEREAS, the City anticipates that this Community Library will serve that purpose.

NOW, THEREFORE, in consideration of the mutual promises contained herein, and other good and valuable consideration, the receipt and adequacy of which is hereby acknowledged, the College and City agree as follows:

1. Principles of Operation.

1.1 The College and City agree to jointly plan, design, construct, furnish, equip, staff, operate and maintain a Community Library on the College's Irving campus on a site to be jointly selected.

1.2 The Irving Public Library will be responsible for managing the day-to-day operations of the Community Library. Current full time professional support staff of the North Lake College Library will be included as staff members of the new Community Library. These employees will work under the general supervision of the Irving Public Library, but will remain employees of the College. Vacancies which occur among full time College employed library professional support staff will be reviewed on an individual basis. The College President and the Irving Public Library Director will agree whether College vacant positions are filled by the College or by the Irving Public Library. In the event of a stalemate on any issue, the college President shall resolve the issue.

1.3 All public space of the Community Library shall be open for common use by College's students, faculty and staff and the general public (hereinafter collectively referred to as the "Users"). All Community Library services shall be offered to all Users on an equal basis. The Library shall be designed and built to ensure compliance with the Americans with Disabilities Act (ADA) and all other laws and regulations.

1.4 The Community Library shall provide quality library service and materials to the Users. Users will have unlimited use of the resources, materials and services of the Community Library subject to the rules and regulations regarding the use and operation of the Library as referenced below.

2. Construction of the Community Library

2.1 The Community Library will consist of a constructed building of not less than 35,000 square feet nor more than 45,000 gross square feet in size with the necessary site improvements including landscaping. The land, building and capital improvements related to the Community Library shall be owned by the College. Ownership of furnishings, equipment and supplies for the Community Library shall be as set forth in Section 3 of this Agreement.

2.2   The College shall provide an amount not to exceed 5.3 Million Dollars ($5,300,000) for the architectural/engineering and related fees, design, plans and specifications, construction documents, construction costs (for all site work, parking, landscaping, and building construction). The College shall provide the site on campus for the Community Library.

2.3   The building plans, design, and specifications will be developed by the College and agreed to by the City. A Building Planning Committee composed of representatives from College and City shall be appointed to work closely with the design and planning professionals from start-to-finish on the project. In the event of a stalemate on any issue, the college President shall resolve the issue. The building and furnishings shall be technologically designed to support computer and electronic data resources.

2.4   The College, in consultation with the City, shall engage the architects. engineers, specialized design professionals, general contractors, sub-contractors and related vendors as necessary for the design, planning and construction of the building, parking and landscaping.

2.5   The Community Library entrance(s) signage will clearly indicate the library's Community affiliation with the College and the City. The design of the exterior and interior signage shall be as mutually agreed between the parties. Signage for the Community Library will be architecturally compatible with rest of campus.

2.6   The Community Library facility shall not be materially altered or modified from its functional purpose. Final decision to materially alter the building rests exclusively with the College.

2.7   The College and the City mutually agree that the name of this library shall be the North Lake Community Library.

3.   **Furnishings/Fixtures/Equipment**
(Refer to Appendix for definition of FFE)

3.1   The City shall provide One Million Nine Hundred Thousand Dollars ($1,900,000) for the interior designer fees, plans and specifications for (FF/E), the purchase of FF/E, and the purchase of an initial collection of library materials to complement the College's existing collection. The College shall utilize the existing College Library's Furnishings Fixtures and Equipment (FF/E) and library materials in the Community Library. Each party shall maintain its own labeling and inventory system for their respective FF/E.

3.2   The City, in consultation with the College, shall engage the interior designers, manufacturers and vendors as necessary for the design, planning and purchase of FF/E for the Community Library.

3.3   The parties shall confer regarding the need and purchase of additional FF/E. New FF/E will be separately purchased by the College and City; each party shall follow its applicable purchasing policies and procedures maintain its own labeling and inventory system. The college President and the City Manager or their respective designees may agree to accept gifts constituting FF/E from any source.

3.4   In the event funding is available for the purchase/commission of public art for the Community Library the art shall be selected as mutually agreed between the College and City.

3.5   Unless otherwise agreed to in writing by the parties, all costs for maintaining and repairing the FF/E for the library shall be borne by the respective owner of such item. Each party shall maintain all FF/E in good repair. In the event that an item has been reported for repair and the responsible party has failed to repair such item within a timely manner such item will be removed from the library and returned to the owner. If such item is necessary for the operation of the library and the removal of such item would negatively affect service of the library then the parties agree to in writing a service schedule and repair.

4.   Materials   Collection

4.1   The materials collection for the Community Library will be broad and general in nature, to complement the academic and general, public library needs. Each library shall be the owner of the materials it brings to or purchases for the Community Library. The College library shall bring its present collection which is valued at $1,195,000 to the new Community Library. The City shall allocate an amount not less than One Million Dollars ($1,000,000) which will be expended over the first three years of this agreement to purchase an initial collection of materials to meet both general public library use and to complement the College library's collection. Both parties shall, subject to appropriation, provide an annual budget allocation for library materials. The parties anticipate the opening collection for the Community Library will exceed 60,000 items.

4.2   The parties shall consult with each other to coordinate the acquisition of new materials including the opening collection so as to best serve the needs of all Users. New materials shall be selected and ordered in accordance with the materials policy of the party that is purchasing the materials.

4.3   Selection of materials shall be consistent with the respective intellectual, academic and First Amendment policies of the respective libraries including due process procedures, if any, for challenged materials.

5. Automation Support Systems
(Refer to appendix for a definition of automation support systems)

5.1   Each party is the owner of their respective data and automated data systems. The parties shall each be responsible for supporting their individual data systems and maintaining the integrity of their data. Neither party shall be liable for any claims, negligent acts, lawsuits, judgments costs and expenses for any damages or loss related to automated data and data systems.. All federal and state laws concerning privacy will be observed by both parties.

5.2   The parties shall consult with each other to do what is feasible and necessary to import/export database records between the Technical Services Department of the College and Irving Public Library automated systems.

5.3   The Community Library's telecommunications, computerized and automated systems and networks shall be designed and installed by the College to provide access to voice, video and data lines for all Users unless otherwise provided in the Community Library's Rules and Regulations.

The Community Library's systems for automated support systems will be designed, installed, and maintained by the College as extensions of the existing college systems and consistent with the standards established for those systems. Equipment and software will be of the same type, quality, and capability as found throughout North Lake College and its use will be consistent with College policies.

Requests for systems, software, or unspecified technology that are not presently supported by the College operations are subject to approval by the Director of Information Systems at North Lake College.

6.   Cataloging/Classification/Processing of Library Materials

6.1   The parties agree that the Library of Congress shall be the classification system used in the Community Library with possible exception of the Irving Public Library's Children's collection which may be classified by the Dewey Decimal System.

6.2   The parties agree that common standards for processing materials will be developed. Each library will order and purchase their respective materials. The Dallas County Community College District Technical Services Center (DCCCD TSC) shall catalog and process all materials purchased by the North Lake College Library per current cost arrangements and shall catalog and process materials purchased by the Irving Public Library for the Community Library at a cost of $5.00 per item. Both parties will review and adjust costs as necessary every two years. Cost increases will be limited to 2% each two years and will not exceed 4% over a six year period. The arrangement shall remain in place for six years, after which a review of the effectiveness and efficiency of the arrangement will be made and a new contract or renewed contract negotiated. Irving will accept the District Standard of Cataloging for the North Lake Community Library.

7.   Management and Staffing

7.1   The organizational structure of the Community Library will be designed to meet the needs of both the College and the City, with as little duplication of services and functions as possible. Clear lines of authority and responsibility will be established consistent with the Agreement as provided in the Community Library's Policies and Procedures to ensure effective management of the Library.

7.2   The parties agree that the Community Library's policies and procedures will include:

   a.   The appointment of a Community Library Manager shall be made by the Irving Public Library subject to the approval of North Lake College. This position shall be responsible for managing, directing and coordinating the activities and services of the library including the supervision of all staff, except the North Lake Library College Head Librarian. The Library Manager shall be liaison with the Irving Public Library and receive general direction from the Irving Public Library Director or his designee. The Head Librarian shall be liaison to the College Library Councils.

   b.   The Head Librarian will work with the Library Manager to develop the overall collection of the Community Library. The Head Librarian's duties will include working with North Lake College faculty and staff to develop the college's library collection and reference services. The Head Librarian will be supervised by the North Lake College Dean of Instructional and Student Support Services or as designated by the college President.

c. The Library Manager will supervise the NLC library professional support staff and the IPL library staff and will administer staff appointments, scheduling, evaluation, training, and staff development. The Library Manager will consult with North Lake College's Dean of Educational Resources on matters of staff appointments, scheduling, evaluation, training, and staff development for college employees. Employees of the City and North Lake College will be managed and evaluated in accordance with their respective institution's personnel procedures and policies..

d. The Library Manager and Head Librarian shall confer at least monthly with the North Lake College Dean of Instructional and Student Support Services or as designated by the college President and the Irving Public Library Assistant Library Director regarding library operational issues. Unresolved issues shall be forwarded to the North Lake College President and Irving Public Library Director for resolution. In the event of a stalemate on any issue, the City Manager and the Chancellor of the College shall resolve the issue.

e. The North Lake Community Library shall meet the standards of the Southern Association of Colleges and Schools.

8. Future Expansion

The parties agree to work cooperatively to implement any future expansion of the Community Library that the parties deem appropriate and necessary to meet the needs of College and City users.

9. Term

9.1 This Agreement shall commence on the date first written above, and shall end 6 years from such date, the "Initial Term", with three (3) six (6) year renewable options, not to exceed a total of twenty four (24) years. Within 365 days before expiration of the Initial Term or any renewal thereof, the parties will negotiate in good faith for the continuation of this Agreement if the parties agree a Community Library is in their best interests. If the parties do not agree, either party may terminate this Agreement upon 180 days written notice to the other party before expiration of the Initial Term or any extension thereof.

10. Costs

10.1   The City of Irving will pay North Lake College a facility use charge of $18,500 per month. Changes in funding for staff loads for either the College or the City will require adjustment to the monthly use fee periodically by mutual written agreement of the parties. (As an example, should the City take over the staffing of a position from the College at a cost of $3,000 per month, the monthly facility use charge would be reduced by that amount. Conversely, should the College take on extra staffing expenses from the City, the monthly facility use charge would be increased by an amount equal to that cost.)

10.2   The parties have analyzed their anticipated operational and maintenance cost of performing their respective duties and obligations under this Agreement. An estimate of these costs is attached as Exhibit A and represents the results of the parties' analysis. The parties generally anticipate this division of costs will result in the College covering approximately forty (40%) percent of the operation and maintenance costs and City covering approximately sixty (60%) percent of the operation and maintenance costs. The parties believe this division of costs is fair and equitable. The parties agree that in the event either party becomes concerned that this division of costs is no longer fair and equitable, and in any event, no less frequently that once every three (3) years, the parties shall meet in good faith to discuss these concerns and to seek to resolve them. Generally, the parties intend that future operational and maintenance cost increases that result in services or improvements that primarily benefit one party should be paid by that party receiving the benefit. If the services or improvements are of generally equal benefit, the cost increase should be shared by the parties.

The division of costs described above is founded, in part, on the anticipated use of the Community Library by the general public as compared to the anticipated use by the College's students, faculty and staff.

10.3   Each party shall keep accurate and comprehensive records of their costs and expenditures associated with meeting their duties and obligations under this Agreement. These records shall be available to the other party within a reasonable time after they are released.

Page 8 of 14 Pages

11. Notice

Whenever a notice is either required or permitted to be given, it shall be given in writing and delivered personally, or delivered by the postal service, certified mail, return receipt requested, to the other party at the address indicated below, or at such other address as may be designated by either party:

If to the College: Office of the President
North Lake College
5001 N. MacArthur
Irving, Texas   75038-3899

If to the City: Office of the City Manager
City of Irving
825 W. Irving Blvd.
Irving, Texas   75015-2288

12. Liability

12.1 The College shall be responsible for any and all claims, damages, liability and court awards including costs, expenses and attorney fees incurred as a result of any action or omission of the College or its officers, employees, and agents in connection with the performance of this Agreement.

12.2 The City shall be responsible for any and all claims, damages, liability and court awards including costs, expenses and attorney fees incurred as a result of any action or omission of the City or its officers, employees, and agents in connection with the performance of this Agreement.

12.3 Nothing in this Section 12 or any other provision of this Agreement shall be construed as a waiver of the notice requirements, defenses, immunities, and limitations the College or City may have under Texas law. The provisions in Section 12 are solely for the benefit of the parties to this Agreement and are not intended to create or grant any rights, contractually or otherwise to any third party.

13. Reporting Third Party Claims

Third party claims are claims submitted by any individual or group who is not a participant in the Agreement between College and City of Irving. For the purpose of this agreement all officers, employees or agents of the participants of this agreement are not considered a third party.

Page 9 of 14 Pages

13.1   The College shall be responsible for responding to any third party claim reported as a result of the alleged negligent condition of the building or grounds.

13.2   The City and the College shall each be responsible for the maintenance and good repair of their individual FF/E. If a third party claim is reported for the alleged negligent use or condition of a FF/E, the owner of the FF/E shall respond to the complaint.

13.3   The City and the College shall each be responsible for the maintenance and data integrity of their individual automated data or data systems and each party shall respond to third party claims involving their respective systems.

13.4   The City and the College shall work together in resolving all third party claims.

14.   Insurance

14.1   Each party shall secure and maintain during the life of this Agreement statutory worker's compensation and liability insurance. Each party shall retain the option of discharging this obligation by means of funded self-insurance.

14.2   The College shall secure and maintain property insurance coverage protecting the Community Library structure and the College's personal property maintained in the Community Library against all risk of physical damage or loss for their full replacement cost. The City shall secure and maintain property insurance protecting the City's personal property maintained in the Community Library for its full replacement cost. College and City hereby mutually waive their respective rights of recovery against each other for any loss insured by property insurance coverage existing for the benefit of the respective parties. Each party may provide this insurance coverage through self-insurance. Any deductibles associated with any insurance provided by either party may be covered through self-insurance.

15.   Default/Remedies

15.1   Except as otherwise provided herein, in the event either party should fail or refuse to perform according to the terms of this Agreement, such party may be declared in default thereof.

15.2 In the event a party has been declared in default hereof, such defaulting party shall be allowed a period of twenty (20) days, from receipt of notice of said default from the nondefaulting party, within which to cure said default. In the event the default remains uncorrected, the nondefaulting party may elect to terminate this Agreement or seek alternate dispute resolution (ADR). But ADR is not binding on the parties. If ADR fails, the parties may seek appropriate legal remedies.

16. Damage and Destruction

16.1 In the event the Community Library is rendered untenable or unfit by fire or other casualty, the parties agree that each shall make its best efforts to identify and recovery any insurance proceeds available for the loss, and apply such proceeds to the repair, restoration or replacement of the Community Library and, if such insurance proceeds are not sufficient, to obtain such additional funds as may be necessary to repair, restore, or replace the Community Library (the "Additional Funds").

16.2 If either party is unable to obtain one-half of the Additional Funds, the other party shall have the option, at its discretion, to make up the shortfall in such funds in order to allow the repair, restoration or replacement to proceed. If the parties are unable to repair or replace the Community Library under the terms of this provision, the Agreement will immediately terminate and no financial obligation shall accrue from the date of such fire or casualty.

17. Non-appropriation

17.1 In the event, the Board of Trustees of the Dallas County Community College District fails to annually appropriate sufficient funds to pay for the College's necessary costs to fulfill its obligations under this Agreement for any College fiscal year, then the College shall consult with the City concerning any reduction in service by the College before any reduction is implemented. If the College reduces services it is obligated to provide under this Agreement due to such non-appropriation, the reduction in services shall be no greater than the reduction in the services for the College's entire North Lake College campus. The reduction of said services shall not constitute a default under this Agreement.

17.2 In the event the City Council of the City of Irving, Texas fails to annually appropriate sufficient funds to pay for the City's necessary costs to fulfill its obligations under this Agreement for any City fiscal year, then the City shall consult with the College concerning any reduction in service by the City before any reduction is implemented. If the City reduces services it is obligated to provide under this Agreement due to such non-appropriation, the reduction in services shall be no greater than the reduction in the same services for the City's entire Irving Public Library system. The reduction of said services shall not constitute a default under this Agreement.

17.3 Each party agrees to timely and properly budget for, request, and pursue the annual appropriation of sufficient funds to meet its obligations hereunder from that party's legislative body(is), and to pursue all available appeals and reviews of any denial or rejection of such requested appropriation.

18. Assignment

Neither the College or City may assign any rights or delegate any duties under this Agreement without the written consent of the other party.

19. Binding Effect

This writing, together with the exhibits hereto, constitutes the entire agreement between the parties' officers, employees, agents and assigns and shall inure to the benefit of their respective survivors, heirs, successors and assigns.

20. Entire Agreement

This Agreement, along with all exhibits and other documents incorporated herein, shall constitute the entire agreement of the parties. Covenants or representations not contained in this Agreement shall not be binding on the parties.

21. Law/Severability

This Agreement shall be governed in all respects by the laws of the State of Texas. In the event any provision of the Agreement shall be held invalid or unenforceable by any court of competent jurisdiction, such holding shall not invalidate or render unenforceable any other provision of this Agreement.

IN WITNESS WHEREOF, the parties have executed this Agreement on the day and year first above written.

For the College:

_____   _____
J. William Wenrich, Chancellor   Date

For the City:

_____   _June 29, 1998_____
Morris Parrish, Mayor   Date

Furniture Fixtures and Equipment (FF/E)

FF/E includes all contents of the Irving Community Library except: the building, automated support systems hardware, telecommunications, multimedia technology, and personal computing equipment.

Automated Support Systems

For the purpose of this agreement, the purchase or lease of personal computing systems equipment, telecommunications, multimedia technology, information systems networks, related support equipment, and the licensing and maintenance of such equipment will be considered part of the automated support systems (see section 5 of the agreement).

All information systems hardware utilized to support the personal computing equipment and software, owned by or leased and maintained by the respective parties to the agreement shall be considered part of the automated support systems.

All software license and maintenance agreements entered into by each respective party to this agreement shall remain between the respective party and their vendor. This agreement does not supersede any other agreement or contract with a third party automated support system vendor.

Software licenses purchased or leased under joint agreement for use at the NLCL shall be installed, maintained and supported by DCCCD. Expanded use allowed by the joint agreement by other IPL sites shall be installed, maintained, and supported by IPL.

North Lake Community Library
Summary Budget Information

NLC – First Year Operating Cost Comparison

	Present	Projected
Salaries & Benefits	$217,887	$217,887
Library Materials	68,000	68,000
Computer Services	72,794	72,794
Operating Costs	42,385	42,385
Maint. & Utilities	73,500	229,484
Addl. Automation Support	0	77,000
Total	**$474,566**	**$707,550**
	Increase of	$232,984

City of Irving – First Year Operating Costs

	General Fund	Bond Fund
Salaries & Benefits	$430,000	
Library Materials	0	$330,000
Materials Processing	56,250	
Misc. Expenses	8,500	
Facility Use Payment	$222,000	
Total	**$716,750**	**$330,000**

6.5.98

Exhibit A
North Lake Community Library
Facilities Operating Expense

Current North Lake Library Facilities Costs
15,000 square foot facility

		Unit Cost	
Landscaping for 1.6 acres		$3,750	$6,000
Contract Janitorial		$1.08	$16,200
Gen. Maintenance & Operations		$1.92	$28,800
Utilities		$1.50	$22,500
	Sub-Total		$73,500

North Lake Community Library Facilities Costs
43,000 square foot facility

		Unit Cost	
Landscaping for 4.8 acres		$3,750	$18,000
Contract Janitorial		$1.08	$46,440
Gen. Maintenance & Operations		$1.92	$82,560
Utilities		$1.50	$64,500
Added College Security Personnel (1 FTE)			$26,400
	Sub-Total		$237,900

North Lake Community Library Other Costs

Extended Automation Support (DCCCD)		$35,000
Extended Automation Support (NLC)		$22,000
	Sub-Total	$57,000
	Total	$294,900
Minus Current NL Library Facilities Costs		$73,500
Total Additional College Costs		$221,400

Exhibit A
North Lake Community Library
Personnel Expenses

	FTE NLC	FTE IPL	FTE Salary	Benefits NLC	Benefits IPL	Budget NLC	Budget IPL	Budget w/Benefits NLC	Budget w/Benefits IPL
Library Services Manager									
Head Librarian - *EC*	0.75	1	$42,756 $60,968	$8,509	$13,253	$60,968	$42,756	$69,477	$56,009
Children's Services									
Children's Librarian		1	$33,408		$11,798		$33,408		$45,206
Senior Library Assistant		1	$24,846		$10,466		$24,846		$35,312
Library Assistant II		1.5	$29,862		$2,283		$29,862		$32,145
Reference Desk									
Senior Librarian		1	$34,254		$11,930		$34,254		$46,184
Reference Librarian (Associate Librarian) - *CV*	0.973		$37,332	$5,673		$37,332		$43,005	
Senior Library Assistant		1	$24,846		$10,466		$24,846		$35,312
Reference Librarian (Assistant Librarian) - *DH*	0.973		$26,544	$4,710		$26,544		$31,254	
Circulation Desk									
Coordinator of Circulation - *KF*	0.937		$22,824	$4,378		$22,824		$27,202	
Circulation Assistant	0.925		$13,000	$1,205		$12,025		$13,230	
Library Assistant I	0.925		$15,267	$1,415		$14,122		$15,537	
Library Assistant II - p/t	1		$16,640	$1,542		$16,640		$18,182	
Library Assistant I - p/t		7.5	$128,610		$9,840		$128,610		$138,450
Administrative Clerk II		1	$19,902		$9,697		$19,902		$29,599
Total Staff Sept. - May	6.5	15.0							
Add For Summer									
Senior Library Assistant		0.25	$6,060		$464		$1,515		$1,979
Library Assistant I		0.25	$4,182		$320		$1,046		$1,366
Totals	6.5	15.5		$27,432	$80,517	$190,455	$341,045	$217,887	$421,562

FTE Ratio = 1:2.5   Expense Ratio = 1:1.8

APPENDIX C
CITY OF IRVING AND
NORTH LAKE COLLEGE
ADDENDUM TO AGREEMENT

 Appendixes available for download as editable Word documents at alaeditions.org/webextras/.

CITY OF IRVING

COUNCIL RESOLUTION NO. 12-17-98- 611

BE IT RESOLVED BY THE CITY COUNCIL OF THE CITY OF IRVING, TEXAS:

SECTION I.   THAT the City Council hereby approves the attached addendum to Section 2.1 of the Intergovernmental Agreement between the City of Irving and the Dallas County Community College District approved by Resolution No. 6-18-98-317 for the development, maintenance, operation and use of a Community Library on the North Lake College campus and the Mayor is authorized to execute said addendum.

SECTION II.   THAT said amendment will increase the maximum size of the library from 45,000 square feet to 55,000 square feet at no additional cost to the City of Irving.

SECTION III.   THAT this resolution shall take effect from and after its final date of passage, and it is accordingly so ordered.

PASSED AND APPROVED BY THE CITY COUNCIL OF THE CITY OF IRVING, TEXAS, this 17th day of December, A.D., 1998.

MORRIS H. PARRISH
MAYOR

ATTEST:

Janice Carroll, CMC
City Secretary

APPROVED AS TO FORM:

Don J. Rorschach
City Attorney

Addendum to
Intergovernmental Agreement and Lease Between the
City of Irving and Dallas County Community College District

This is an Addendum to the Intergovernmental Agreement and Lease Between the City of Irving and Dallas County Community College District, approved by Irving City Council Resolution No. 6-18-98-317 and entered into by and between the City of Irving, Texas, and Dallas County Community College District. The parties hereto agree to amend Section 2.1 of the agreement to increase the minimum/maximum square footage of the Community Library from 35,000-45,000 square feet to 45,000-55,000 square feet which amended section shall read as follows and there shall not be any additional cost to the City of Irving:

2.1 The Community Library will consist of a constructed building of not less than 45,000 square feet nor more than 55,000 gross square feet in size with the necessary site improvements including landscaping. The land, building and capital improvements related to the Community Library shall be owned by the College. Ownership of furnishings, equipment and supplies for the Community Library shall be as set forth in Section 3 of this Agreement.

CITY OF IRVING, TEXAS

By: _____
Morris H. Parrish, Mayor

ATTEST:

_____
Janice Carroll, CMC
City Secretary

APPROVED AS TO FORM:

_____
Don J. Rorschach
City Attorney

**DALLAS COUNTY COMMUNITY
COLLEGE DISTRICT**

By: _____
J. William Wenrich, Chancellor

ATTEST:

_____

APPROVED AS TO FORM:

_____
Robert Young, Attorney for the Dallas
County Community College District

Approved 12-17-98
Resolution #12-17-98-611

MAYOR'S ACKNOWLEDGMENT

THE STATE OF TEXAS §
COUNTY OF DALLAS §

    BEFORE ME, the undersigned authority, a Notary Public in and for said County and State, on this day personally appeared Morris H. Parrish, Mayor of the City of Irving, Texas, a municipal corporation, known to me to be the person and officer whose name is subscribed to the foregoing instrument and acknowledged to me that the same was the act of the said City of Irving, Texas, a municipal corporation, that he was duly authorized to perform the same by appropriate resolution of the City Council of the City of Irving and that he executed the same as the act of the said City for purpose and consideration therein expressed, and in the capacity therein stated.

    GIVEN UNDER MY HAND AND SEAL OF OFFICE this 22 day of December, A.D., 199 8.

_____
Notary Public In and For the State of Texas

My Commission Expires:

8-25-2001

CORPORATE ACKNOWLEDGMENT

THE STATE OF TEXAS §
COUNTY OF DALLAS §

    BEFORE ME, the undersigned authority, a Notary Public in and for said County and State, on this day personally appeared J. William Wenrich, Chancellor of Dallas County Community College District known to me to be the person and officer whose name is subscribed to the foregoing instrument and acknowledged to me that the same was the act of the Dallas County Community College District, that he was duly authorized to perform the same by appropriate resolution of the board of directors of such district and that he executed the same as the act of the said district for purposes and consideration therein expressed, and in the capacity therein stated.

    GIVEN UNDER MY HAND AND SEAL OF OFFICE this 12 day of January, A.D., 199 9.

_____
Notary Public In and For the State of Texas

My Commission Expires:

5/29/02

MARIA E. SANCHEZ
MY COMMISSION EXPIRES
May 29, 2002

REFERENCES

Achen, Paris. 2003. "Cy-Fair College Teams with County." *Chron.com. Houston Chronicle.* June 19, 1–3. http:chron.com.

Albanese, Andrew. 2007. "Revisions to Nova U.—Broward County Library Agreement Will Save County $1.7 Million." *Library Journal,* October 16. http://www.libraryjournal.com/article/CA6491485.html.

Anderson, Susan. 1999. "Planning for the Future: Combining a Community and College Library." *Library Administration & Management* 13, no. 2: 81–86.

Anderson Brulé Architects, Inc. 2005. *Virginia Beach Lifelong Learning Center: Joint-Use Library Feasibility Analysis: Final Report.* San Jose: Anderson Brulé Architects, Inc. November 4. http://www.vbgov.com/file_source/dept/library/Library%20Special%20Projects/joint%20use%201ibrary/Document/final_vb_llc_feasibility_analysis_0604.pdf..

"Anderson Brulé Architects' Decision to Stay Small Brought Bigger Opportunities for Work." 2010. *Silicon Valley/San Jose Business Journal,* August 22. http://www.bizjournals.com/sanjose/stories/2010/08/23/smallb4.html.

Bauer, Patricia T. 2006. "Changing Places: Personnel Issues of Joint Use Library in Transition." *Library Trends* 54, no. 4: 581–95.

Berinstein, Paula. 2006. "Wikipedia and Britannica." *Searcher.* March 16–26. http://ebscohost.com.

Berry, John. 1996. "Gale Research Inc. Library of the Year 1996: Broward County Library." *Library Journal*, June 15: 28–31.

———. 2004. "Gale/LJ Library of the Year 2004: San José Public Library & San José State University Library—The San José Model." *Library Journal.com*, June 15. http://www.libraryjournal.com/article/CA423793.html.

Bostick, Sharon. 2001. "Academic Library Consortia in the United States: An Introduction." *Liber Quarterly* 11: 6–13.

Breivik, Patricia Senn, Luann Budd, and Richard F. Woods. 2005. "We're Married! The Rewards and Challenges of Joint Libraries." *Journal of Academic Librarianship* 31, no. 5: 401–8.

Broward College. 2008. "News and Announcements: Broward College, County, NSU Open Miramar Library." http://www.broward.edu/student/AnnouncementsStudent/page21712.html.

Broward County Library System. 2010. "Broward County Library Timeline." Broward County Library System. http://www.browardlibrary.org/web/BCL_Timeline.pdf.

Bundy, Alan. 2003. "Joint-Use Libraries—The Ultimate Form of Cooperation." In *Planning the Modern Public Library Building* edited by Gerard B. McCabe and James R. Kennedy. Westport, CT: Libraries Unlimited. http://www.library.unisa .edu.au/about/papers/jointuse.pdf .

Bundy, Alan, and Larry Amey. 2006. "Libraries Like No Others: Evaluating the Performance and Progress of Joint Use Libraries." *Library Trends* 54, no. 4: 501–18. http://www.ideals.illinois.edu/bitstream/handle/2142/3644/BundyAmey 544.pdf?sequence=2.

California Postsecondary Education Commission. 2011. "Facilities Review: Joint Use Educational Centers." Sacramento, CA: California Postsecondary Education Commission. http://www.cpec.ca.gov/Reviews/FacilityReviewJointUse.asp.

California State Library. 2000. *Public and School Libraries: Issues and Options of Joint Use Facilities and Cooperative Use Agreements.* Sacramento, CA: California State Library.

"Canyon Gate Communities Press Releases: The New Harris County LibraryAdds Educational Opportunities for Stone Gate Residents." 2004. Canyon Gate Communities/Land Tejas Companies, November 13. http://www.canyongate.com/media/pressreleases/index.php?id=26.

CCS Partnerships. 2011. "Collaborative Practices: Joint Use." Sacramento, CA: CCS Partnership. http://www.ccspartnership.org/T_collaborativeP_jointUse.cfm.

Center for Cities and Schools. 2010. *Partnerships for Joint Use: Expanding the Use of Public School Infrastructure to Benefit Students and Communities: Research Report: Executive Summary.* Berkeley: University of California Berkeley, September. http://citiesandschools.berkeley.edu/reports/Partnerships_JU_Aug2010_exec_sum.pdf.

City of Irving. 2005. *Comprehensive Plan Update.* City of Irving. http://www.ci.irving
.tx.us/planning-and-inspections/pdfs/comprehensive-plan-updated-report.pdf .

City of Lincoln, Western Placer Unified School District, and Sierra Joint Community
College District. 2003. *Joint Use Cooperative Agreement for the Lincoln Public
Library at Twelve Bridges.* City of Lincoln, Western Placer Unified School District,
and Sierra Joint Community College District, March 11. http://www.library.ca.gov/
lba2000/c2appdocs/LincolnBuildingProgram.pdf.

City of Sacramento, Sacramento Public Library Authority, Natomas Unified School
District, and Los Rios Community College District. 2000. *Cooperative Agree-
ment: Library for North Natomas.* City of Sacramento, Sacramento Public
Library Authority, Natomas Unified School District, and Los Rios Community
College District. http://www.library.ca.gov/lba2000/c3appdocs/NorthNatomas
JointUseAgreement.pdf.

City of Virginia Beach. 2011. *Fact Sheet—Joint Use Library: City of Virginia Beach
and Tidewater Community College.* Virginia Beach, VA: City of Virginia Beach,
http://www.vbgov.com/file_source/dept/library/Library%20Special%20Projects/
joint%20use%20library/Document/Jointuselibraryfactsheet.pdf.

Coconino Community College. 2010. "News: NAU and CCC Announce New Library
Partnership." http://www.coconino.edu/Lists/News/DispForm.aspx?ID=21.

Cole Library. 2011. "Mount Vernon Public Library: One-of-a-Kind Library." http://
colelibrary.org/oneofakind.shtml.

Cornell University Library. 2011. "News: Columbia and Cornell Announce New
Partnership." http://www.library.cornell.edu/news/091012/2cul.

Crawford, Walt. 2003. "The Philosophy of Joint-Use Libraries." *American Libraries*
34, no. 11: 83.

Cy-Fair Houston Chamber of Commerce. 2008. "News: Troyer Leaves an Impressive
Legacy as She Embarks on New Career Venture." Cy-Fair Houston Chamber of
Commerce, September. http://www.cyfairchamber.com/September2008.html.

Dalton, Pete, Judith Elkin, and Anne Hannaford. 2006. "Joint Use Libraries as
Successful Strategic Alliances." *Library Trends* 54, no. 4: 535–48.

Davenport, Nancy. 2006. "Place as Library?" *Educause Reviews* 41, no. 1: 12–13.
http://net.educause.edu/ir/library/pdf/erm0616.pdf.

Dornseif, Karen. 2001. "Joint-Use Libraries: Balancing Autonomy and Cooperation."
In *Joint Use Libraries,* edited by William Miller and Rita M. Pellen, 103–16. New
York: Haworth Information.

Dornseif, Karen, and Ken Draves. 2003. "The Joint-Use Library: The Ultimate
Collaboration." *Colorado Libraries* 29, no. 1: 5–8.

Downing, Margaret. 2002. "The Old West: He Looks Like Clint Eastwood and
Loves John Wayne; Now This County Official Faces a Showdown with Tomball's

Elderly." *Houston Press,* August 22. http://www.houstonpress.com/content/printVersion/226732/.

Eanes, Joel. 2010. "The San Jose Joint Library: The Development of a Joint City/University Library." Master's thesis, San Jose State University. http://scholarworks.sjsu.edu/cgi/viewcontent.cgi?article=4803&context=etd_theses&sei-redir=1#search="eanes+master+theses+san+jose=state+2010.

Feighan, Maureen. 2009. "Macomb Library Will Stop Lending Books: Wayne State to Take Over Building." *The Detroit News,* April 18. http://detnews.com/article/20090418/METRO/904180349/Macomb-library-will-stop-lending-books.

Florida Postsecondary Education Planning Commission. 1999. *Impact of Joint Use Facilities on the Delivery of Postsecondary Education in Florida.* Tallahassee, FL, December. http://www.cepri.state.fl.us/pdf/jointuse_cvr.pdf.

Fort Collins Regional Library District. 2007. "Intergovernmental Agreement among Fort Collins Regional Library District, City of Fort Collins, Colorado and the County of Larimer, Colorado." December 18. http://www.poudrelibraries.org/about/pdf/iga-final.pdf.

Freeman, Geoffrey T. 2005. *Library as Place: Rethinking Roles, Rethinking Space: Perspectives on the Evolving Library.* Washington, DC: Council on Library and Information Resources.

Fugate, Cynthia. 2001. "Common Ground: Making Library Services Work at a Collocated Campus." In *Joint Use Libraries,* edited by William Miller and Rita M. Pellen, 55–64. New York: Haworth Information.

Garrow, Hattie Brown. 2005. "Study Says TCC, City Library Would Benefit Community." *Virginian Pilot,* December 15, V3. http://infotrac.com.

Gaskins, Rosa M. 2004. "Joint-Use Libraries: A Personal Account." *Community & Junior College Libraries* 13, no. 1: 37–43.

Green, Susan, and Claire Gunnels. 2005. "Voices from the Trenches: Librarians Reflect on the Joint-Use Library." *Community & Junior College Libraries* 13, no. 3: 25–31.

Guernsey, Lisa. 1998. "Should a College and a City Share a Single Library?" *The Chronicle of Higher Education,* October 30: A25. http://chronicle.com.lscsproxy.lonestar.edu/article/Should-a-Collegea-City/25012/.

Gunnels, Claire. 2009. *LIFE in the Library: Events to Build Community.* Morrisville, NC: Lulu.

Halverson, Kathleen, and Jean Plotas. 2006. "Creating and Capitalizing on the Town/Gown Relationship: An Academic Library and a Public Library Form a Community Partnership." *Journal of Academic Librarianship* 32, no. 6: 624–29.

Haycock, Ken. 2006. "Dual-Use Libraries: Guidelines for Success." *Library Trends* 54, no. 4: 488–500.

Henderson, Everett, Kim A. Miller, Terri Craig, Suzanne Dorinski, Michael Freeman, Natasha Isaac, Jennifer Keng Pierson, Patricia O'Shea, and Peter Schilling. 2011. *Public Libraries in the United States Fiscal Year 2008.* Washington, DC: Institute of

Library and Museum Studies. http://harvester.census.gov/imls/pubs/pls/pub_detail
.asp?id=130.

Hennen, Thomas J. 2002. "Joint Library Issues for Wisconsin Libraries." Waukeha
County Federated Library System. January 15. http://www.srlaaw.org/documents/
JointLibrary.pdf.

Johnson, Marilyn. 2010. "We Will All Feel the Loss from Cuts to Our Libraries."
Houston Chronicle, July 8, B9.

Kauppila, Paul, Sandra E. Belanger, and Lisa Rosenblum. 2007. "Merge Everything
It Makes Sense to Merge: The History and Philosophy of the Merged Reference
Collection at the Dr. Martin Luther King, Jr. Library in San Jose, California."
Collection Management 31, no. 3: 33–57. doi:10.1300/J105v31n03_04.

Kauppila, Paul, and Sharon Russell. 2003. "Economies of Scale in the Library World:
The Dr. Martin Luther King Jr. Library in San Jose, California." *New Library World*
104, nos. 7/8: 255–66.

King, Sally, and John Presley. 1995. "The Cooperative Concept: Worthy of Consideration." *Virginia Librarian* 41, no. 3: 19–22.

Kowba, William A. 2011. "Letter Regarding 2010/2011 Grand Jury Report: Library
Charter School Filed April 11, 2011." July 11. http://www.sdcounty.ca.gov/
grandjury/reports/2010-2011/LibraryCharterSchoolFinalReport_response1.pdf.

KPMG. 2006. *Shared Services in the Higher Education Sector: Report to HEFCE.*
London: Higher Education Funding Council for England. July. http://www
.kingstoncitygroup.co.uk/includes/docs/library/shared/Shared%20Service%
20in%20Higher%20Education%20KPMG%20report.pdf.

Kratz, Charles. 2003. "Transforming the Delivery of Service: The Joint-Use Library and
Information Commons." *College & Research Libraries News* 64, no. 2: 100–101.

Kurzweil, Ray. 2005. *The Singularity Is Near: When Humans Transcend Biology.* New
York: Viking.

Lafayette Library and Learning Center. 2011. "Glenn Seaborg Learning Consortium."
http://www.lafayettelib.org/consortium/.

Leighton, Philip D., and David C. Weber. 1999. *Planning Academic and Research
Library Buildings.* 3rd ed. Chicago: American Library Association.

Light, Jane. 2008. "Opening King: A Joint Library Venture." *California of the Past:
Digital Story Station.* San Diego, CA: California State Library Media Arts Center
and San Jose Public Library. http://blip.tv/san-jose-stories/opening-king-a-joint
-library-venture-by-jane-light-4191423.

Lubans, John. 2002. "A Portrait of Collaborative Leadership: Donald E. Riggs and
Nova Southeastern University's Joint-Use Library." *Library Administration &
Management* 16, no. 4: 176–78.

MacDougall, Harriet D., and Nora J. Quinlan. 2001. "Staffing Challenges for a Joint
Use Library: The Nova Southeastern University and Broward County Experience."

In *Joint Use Libraries*, edited by William Miller and Rita M. Pellen, 131–50. New York: Haworth Information.

Macomb County Research and Reference Center. 2011. "MCRRC Home Page– Macomb County Research and Reference Center." http://www.libcoop.net/mcl/.

Marie, Kirsten L. 2007. "One Plus One Equals Three: Joint Use Libraries in Urban Areas—The Ultimate Form of Library Cooperation." *Library Administration & Management* 21, no. 1: 23–28.

Martin, Elizabeth, and Brian Kenney. 2004. "Library Buildings 2004: Great Libraries in the Making." *Library Journal*, December 15. http://www.libraryjournal.com/article/ CA485757.html.

Matthews, Rosemary. 2009. "Emmetsburg Community Service: Libraries—Combined Libraries." http://www.emmetsburg.com/Community/Libraries.htm.

McMenemy, David. 2009. *The Public Library.* London: Facet.

McNicol, Sarah. 2006. "What Makes a Joint Use Library a Community Library?" *Library Trends* 54, no. 4: 519–34.

Miller, Claire Cain, and Julie Bosman. 2011. "E-Books Outsell Print Books at Amazon." *New York Times*, May 20, B2. http://search.proquest.com/docview/867703628 ?accountid=7054.

Miller, William. 2003. "Joint-Use Libraries: Sharing Facilities for Greater Efficiency." *Library Issues* 24, no. 2: 1–4.

Minnesota Library Development and Services. 2000. *Jointly Operated School and Public Library Services in the Same Location: Co-Location: A Guide to Community Based Library Services.* Roseville, MN: Minnesota Department of Education.

New Jersey Association of School Librarians, New Jersey Library Association, and New Jersey State Library. 2003. *School/Public Library Joint Use Facility Standards.* New Jersey Library Association. http://www.njasl.org/documents/GuidelinesforJoint School-PublicLibraries_000.pdf.

New Jersey Library Association. 2002. "Public Libraries and School Libraries: Perfect Together?" New Jersey Library Association. November 26. http://www.njla.org/ statements/jointpubschool.html.

New Schools/Better Neighborhoods. 2003. "Case Studies: Joint Use Facilities." New Schools/Better Neighborhoods. http://www.nsbn.org/case/jointuse/sacschool partnership.php.

North Harris Montgomery Community College District, Board of Trustees. 2002. "Financial Report and Consideration No. 6. (ACTION ITEM 7)." Board Meeting of the North Harris Montgomery Community College District. April 30.

———. 2002. "Financial Report and Consideration No. 20 (ACTION ITEM 20)." Board Meeting of the North Harris Montgomery Community College District. January 22.

Nova Southeastern University. 2011. "Alvin Sherman Library, Research, and Information Technology Center, a Joint-Use Facility with the Broward County Board of Commissioners." Nova Southeastern University. http://www.nova.edu/library/main/.

Olliver, James, and Susan Anderson. 2001. "Seminole Community Library—Joint-Use Library Services for the Community and the College." *Resource Sharing & Information Networks* 15, no. 1: 89–102. http://www.informaworld.com/10.1300/J121v15n01_07.

Park, Catherine S. 2005. "Joint Use Libraries: Are They Really Worth the Challenges?" *Texas Library Journal* 81, no. 1: 6, 8–10.

Park, Cathy, Judy Murray, and Earl Campa. 2007. "Joint Use Libraries: Agony and Ecstasy." (PowerPoint presentation). Harris County Public Library.

"Parking Garages Come to the Suburbs." 2001. *Constructive Advice.* Spring. http://www.highconstruction.com/hcc/Resources/ConstructiveAdvice/2001Spring/parkinggarages.html?nav=true.

Peterson, Christina A. 2005. "Space Designed for Lifelong Learning: The Dr. Martin Luther King Jr. Joint-Use Library." In *Library as Place: Rethinking Roles, Rethinking Space*, CLIR Pub. 129 (February). Washington, DC: Council on Library and Information Resources. http://www.clir.org/pubs/reports/pub129/peterson.html.

Queensland Government, Department of Education. 1996. *Guidelines for the Development of Joint-Use School Community Libraries.* Queensland, Australia: Queensland Department of Education. http://education.qld.gov.au/library/docs/joint-use.

Quinlan, Nora J., and Johanna Tuñón. 2004. "Providing Reference in a Joint-Use Library." In *Improving Internet Reference Services to Distance Learners*, edited by William Miller and Rita M. Pellen, 111–28. Binghamton: Haworth Information.

Reicher, Mike. 2011. "Tomes' Time Might Be Up at Newport Beach Library." *Los Angeles Times*, March 29. http://articles.latimes.com/2011/apr/01/local/la-me-0329-newport-library-20110329.

Reno, Eric E. 1999. "Joint-Use Libraries: A College President's Perspective." *Colorado Libraries* 25, no. 2: 10–11.

Richmond County Public Library. 1998. "Memorandum of Understanding between RCC and Richmond County." Richmond County Public Library, September 10. http://www.rcplva.org/about us/TSTDLC%20RPCL%20Board%200f%20Trustees/memorandum-of-understanding-between-rcc-and-richmond-county.html.

Riggs, Donald E. 2000. Editorial: "Joint-Use Libraries: Thinking Out of the Box." *College and Research Libraries* 61, no. 2: 96–97. http://www.ala.org/ala/acrl/acrlpubs/crljournal/backissues2000b/march00/candrlmarch2000editorial.htm.

Rockman, I. F. 1999. "Joint Use Facilities: The View from San Jose: An Interview with C. James Schmidt." *Library Administration & Management* 13, no. 2: 64–67.

San Diego Grand Jury 2010/2011. 2011. "Library Charter School: The Law of Unintended Consequences." April 11. http://www.sdcounty.ca.gov/grandjury/reports/2010-2011/LibraryCharterSchoolFinalReport.pdf.

"San José City Council Defers Library-Filter Mandate." 2009. *American Libraries,* May 1. http://www.ala.org/ala/alonline/currentnews/newsarchive/2009/may2009/sanjosedefersfilters50109.cfm.

"San Jose Library's Filter Report Not Enough for City Councilor." 2008. *American Libraries,* May 16. http://www.ala.org/ala/alonline/currentnews/newsarchive/2008/may2008/sanjosecouncilmanwantsfilters.cfm.

Schiff, Stacy. 2006. "Know It All: Can Wikipedia Conquer Expertise?" *New Yorker,* July 31: 36. http://www.newyorker.com/archive/2006/07/31/060731fa_fact.

Schmidt, Eric. 2005. "Books of Revelation." *Wall Street Journal.* October 18: A18. http://proquest.com.

Schwanz, Kathleen. 2000. "Thinking about a Joint-Use Library? A Memorandum of Agreement and Timetable Can Ensure Success." *College & Research Libraries News* 61, no. 6: 478–80. http://www.ala.org/ala/acrl/acrlpubs/crlnews/backissues2000/june2/thinkingabout.htm.

Sherman, Amy. 2007. "NSU Library Remains Open to Nonstudents: Broward County and NSU Have Closed the Books on Their Library Tiff, Ensuring Public Access." *Miami Herald,* October 3. http://web.ebscohost.com.

Shorten, Jay, Michele Seikel, and Janet H. Ahrberg. 2005. "Why Do You Still Use Dewey?" *Library Resources & Technical Services* 49, no. 2: 123–36.

Shupe, Sam. 2009. "A Tale of Two Colleges: Bye-Bye to CC?" *Husky Herald.* November 5. http://www.huskyherald.com/2009/11/05/a-tale-of-two-colleges-bye-bye-to-cc/.

Smith, Veronica. 2006. "A Further Perspective on Joint Partnerships: A Commentary on Creating and Capitalizing on the Town/Gown Relationship." *Journal of Academic Librarianship* 32, no. 6: 630–31.

State Library of Iowa. 2006. *Is a Combined School/Public Library Right for Your Community? A Guide for Decision Makers.* Des Moines, IA. http://www.statelibraryofiowa.org/ld/q-s/school-librarians/combined-sch-pl/guide.

Stubbs, Ryan, and Andy Carlson. 2007. *Front Range Community College-Larimer Campus Facilities Master Plan: Agenda Item II C.* Denver, CO: Colorado Commission on Higher Education. November 1. http://highered.colorado.gov/CCHE/Meetings/2007/nov/nov07iic.pdf .

Sullivan, Kathy, Warren Taylor, Mary Grace Barrick, and Roger Stelk. 2006. "Building the Beginnings of a Beautiful Partnership. *Library Trends* 54, no. 4: 569–80.

Tippecanoe County/Ivy Tech Library. 2002. *Tippecanoe County Public Library Ivy Tech State College Joint-Use Library Project Proposal.* Tippecanoe County Library. Revised April 10. http://www.tcpl.lib.in.us/branch/proposal.htm.

Trombley, William, and Carl Irving. 2001. "Co-Location Experiment: Ten Year Old University Branch and a Community College Share a Campus." *National CrossTalk* 9, no. 1: 9–10.

University of Washington Bothell, Cascadia Community College. 2011. "Campus Library Borrowing Services." University of Washington Bothell Campus Library. http://library.uwb.edu/circ.html#placehold.

Urban Libraries Council. 2010. "Member Innovations 2010: Glenn Seaborg Learning Consortium (GSLC) Contra Costa County Library, CA." Urban Libraries Council. http://urbanlibraries.org/displaycommon.cfm?an=1&subarticlenbr=305.

Virginia Beach Lifelong Learning Center. *Joint-Use Library Feasibility Analysis*. 2005. Tidewater Community College. Final Report. November 5. http://www.vbgov.com/file_source/dept/library/Library%20Special%20Projects/joint%20use%20library/Document/final_vb_llc_feasibility_analysis_0604.pdf.

Wagner, Lon. 2009. "Ideas, Hopes Pitched for City and College's $53 M Library Project." *Virginian Pilot*, March 17, B2. http://infotrac.com.

Walter, Scott. 2010. "Advocacy through Engagement: Public Engagement and the Academic Library." In *Advocacy, Outreach, and the Nation's Academic Libraries: A Call for Action*, edited by W. C. Welburn, J. Simmons-Welburn, and B. McNeil, 3–42. Chicago: Association of College and Research Libraries.

Williams, Bob. 2002. RE: Library Contract, Draft of Agenda Item. E-mail communication to Sandra McMullan. North Harris Montgomery Community College District, October 28.

Wisconsin, Department of Public Instruction, Division for Library Services. 1998. *Combined School and Public Libraries: Guidelines for Decision Making*. 2nd ed. Madison, WI: Wisconsin Department of Public Instruction's Division for Library Services. http://dpi.wi.gov/pld/comblibs.html.

Woods, Julia A. 2001. "Joint-Use Libraries: The Broward Community College Central Campus Experience." In *Joint Use Libraries*, edited by William Miller and Rita M. Pellen, 41–53. New York: Haworth Information.

Woods, Richard F. 2004. "Sharing Technology for a Joint-Use Library." *Resource Sharing & Information Networks* 17, nos. 1/2: 205–20.

Wright, Francesca. 2005. "City of Lincoln, Placer County, CA: Joint Facilities Planning, Construction and Use." In *Stretching Community Dollars: Cities, Counties and School Districts Building for the Future*. Sacramento: Community School Partnerships. http://www.ccspartnership.org/caseStudies/2005/Lincoln.pdf.

INDEX

ABOUT THE AUTHORS

Claire Gunnels is founding faculty and assistant director of the Lone Star College-CyFair Branch Library, a joint library with Harris County Public Library in Houston, Texas. She is the author of *LIFE in the Library: Events to Build Community* (2009) and writes occasionally for *Community & Junior College Libraries*. Gunnels earned her bachelor's degree in history from Mount Holyoke College and her master's degree in library science from Simmons College.

Susan Green came to Lone Star College-CyFair Branch Library as founding faculty. Previously, she served as branch manager for the Maud Marks branch of Harris County Public Library. She has written for *Community & Junior College Libraries* and *Inquiry.* She earned her bachelor's degree in business administration from Washington University in St. Louis, her master's in business administration from the University of Texas at Arlington, and her master's in library science from the University of North Texas.

Patricia Butler started her professional career as an archivist for the Colonial Williamsburg Foundation after graduating from the University of North Texas with a bachelor's degree in history. She earned her master's degree in library and information sciences from the Catholic University of America. She later served as a librarian for the Virginia Department for the Deaf and Hard of Hearing, a reference/instruction librarian at the Manassas Campus of Northern Virginia Community College, and from 2002 until 2009, as a reference librarian at the Lone Star College-Tomball Community Library.